# F8

Paper F8
Audit and
Assurance
(INT and UK)

Study Manual

ACCA

British Library Cataloguing-in-Publication Data
A catalogue record for this book is available from the British Library

Published by InterActive World Wide Limited
Westgate House, 8-9 Holborn
London EC1N 2LL

**www.iaww.com**
**www.studyinteractive.org**

ISBN 978-1-907217-55-5

Second Edition 2010
Printed in Romania

# Foreword

Thank you for choosing to study with the London School of Business and Finance (LSBF).

A dynamic, quality-oriented and innovative educational institution, the London School of Business and Finance offers specialised programmes, designed with students and employers in mind. We are always at the frontline driving the latest professional developments and trends.

LSBF attracts the highest quality candidates from over 140 countries worldwide. We work in partnership with leading accountancy firms, banks and best-practice organisations – enabling thousands of students to realise their full potential in accountancy, finance and the business world.

With an international perspective, LSBF has developed a rich portfolio of professional qualifications and executive education programmes. To complement our face-to-face and cutting-edge online learning products, LSBF is now pleased to offer tailored study materials to support students in their preparation for exams.

The exam focused content in this manual will provide you with a comprehensive and up-to-date understanding of the ACCA syllabus. We have an award-winning team of tutors, who are highly experienced in helping students through their professional exams and have received consistently excellent feedback.

I hope that you will find this manual helpful and wish you the best of luck in your studies.

**Aaron Etingen**

ACCA, MSI, Founder and CEO

# Contents

London
School of Business
& Finance

shaping success in business and finance

# F8

## About ACCA
## Paper F8 -
## Audit and
## Assurance
## (INT and UK)

London
School of Business
& Finance

shaping success in business and finance

# Aim of the Exam Paper

The aim of the paper is to develop knowledge and understanding of the process of carrying out the assurance engagement, and its application in the context of the professional regulatory framework.

# Outline of the Syllabus

1. Audit framework and regulation
2. Internal audit
3. Planning and risk assessment
4. Internal control
5. Audit evidence
6. Review
7. Reporting

# Format of the Exam Paper

The syllabus is assessed by a three hour paper-based examination consisting of five compulsory questions. The bulk of the questions will be discursive but some questions involving computational elements will be set from time to time.

The questions will cover all areas of the syllabus:

- Question 1 will be a scenario-based question worth 30 marks.
- Question 2 will be a knowledge-based question worth 10 marks.
- Questions 3, 4 and 5 will be worth 20 marks each.

# Getting the most from your studies

Manage your time effectively. If you have a busy work schedule use your study planner to catch up. Do not allow yourself to fall behind.

Make sure that you can apply all the numbers to the formulae and can perform the calculations accurately.

Practice as many questions as you can. You should aim to have attempted every question in the revision kit at least twice before the exam.

London
School of Business
& Finance

shaping success in business and finance

# F8

## Syllabus and
## Study Guide

# Audit and Assurance (INT)

This syllabus and study guide is designed to help with planning study and to provide detailed information on what could be assessed in any examination session.

# The Structure of the Syllabus and Study Guide

RELATIONAL DIAGRAM OF PAPER WITH OTHER PAPERS

This diagram shows direct and indirect links between this paper and other papers preceding or following it. Some papers are directly underpinned by other papers such as Advanced Performance Management by Performance Management. These links are shown as solid line arrows. Other papers only have indirect relationships with each other such as links existing between the accounting and auditing papers. The links between these are shown as dotted line arrows. This diagram indicates where you are expected to have underpinning knowledge and where it would be useful to review previous learning before undertaking study.

OVERALL AIM OF THE SYLLABUS

This explains briefly the overall objective of the paper and indicates in the broadest sense the capabilities to be developed within the paper.

MAIN SECTIONS

This paper's aim is broken down into several main sections which divide the syllabus and study guide.

RELATIONAL DIAGRAM OF THE MAIN SECTIONS

This diagram illustrates the flows and links between the main sections of the syllabus and should be used as an aid to planning teaching and learning in a structured way.

SYLLABUS RATIONALE

This is a narrative explaining how the syllabus is structured and how the main capabilities are linked. The rationale also explains in further detail what the examination intends to assess and why.

DETAILED SYLLABUS

This shows the breakdown of the main capabilities (sections) of the syllabus into subject areas. This is the blueprint for the detailed study guide

APPROACH TO EXAMINING THE SYLLABUS

This section briefly explains the structure of the examination and how it is assessed.

STUDY GUIDE

This is the main document that students, tuition providers and publishers should use as the basis of their studies, instruction and materials. Examinations will be based on the detail of the study guide which comprehensively identifies what could be assessed in any examination session. The study guide is a precise reflection and breakdown of the syllabus. It is divided into sections based on the main capabilities identified in the syllabus. These sections are divided into subject areas which relate to the sub-capabilities included in the detailed syllabus. Subject areas are broken down into sub-headings which describe the detailed outcomes that could be assessed in examinations. These outcomes are described using verbs indicating what exams may require students to demonstrate, and the broad intellectual level at which these may need to be demonstrated (see intellectual levels overleaf).

# Intellectual Levels

The syllabus is designed to progressively broaden and deepen the knowledge, skills and professional values demonstrated by the student on their way through the qualification.

The specific capabilities within the detailed syllabuses and study guides are assessed at one of three intellectual or cognitive levels:

Level 1:    Knowledge and comprehension;
Level 2:    Application and analysis;
Level 3:    Synthesis and evaluation.

Very broadly, these intellectual levels relate to the three cognitive levels at which the Knowledge module, the Skills module and the Professional level are assessed.

Each subject area in the detailed study guide included in this document is given a 1, 2, or 3 superscript, denoting intellectual level, marked at the end of each relevant line. This gives an indication of the intellectual depth at which an area could be assessed within the examination. However, while level 1 broadly equates with the Knowledge module, level 2 equates to the Skills module and level 3 to the Professional level, some lower level skills can continue to be assessed as the student progresses through each module and level. This reflects that at each stage of study there will be a requirement to broaden, as well as deepen capabilities. It is also possible that occasionally some higher level capabilities may be assessed at lower levels.

# Learning Hours

The ACCA qualification does not prescribe or recommend any particular number of learning hours for examinations because study and learning patterns and styles vary greatly between people and organisations. This also recognises the wide diversity of personal, professional and educational circumstances in which ACCA students find themselves.

Each syllabus contains between 23 and 35 main subject area headings depending on the nature of the subject and how these areas have been broken down.

# Guide to Exam Structure

The structure of examinations varies within and between modules and levels.

The Fundamentals level examinations contain 100% compulsory questions to encourage candidates to study across the breadth of each syllabus.

The Knowledge module is assessed by equivalent two-hour paper based and computer based examinations.

The Skills module examinations are all paper based three-hour papers. The structure of papers varies from 10 questions in the Corporate and Business Law (F4) paper to four 25 mark questions in Financial Management (F9). Individual questions within all Skills module papers will attract between 10 and 30 marks.

The Professional level papers are all three-hour paper based examinations, all containing two sections. Section A is compulsory, but there will be some choice offered in Section B.

For all three hour examination papers, ACCA has introduced 15 minutes reading and planning time.

This additional time is allowed at the beginning of each three-hour examination to allow candidates to read the questions and to begin planning their answers before they start writing in their answer books. This time should be used to ensure that all the information and exam requirements are properly read and understood.

During reading and planning time candidates may only annotate their question paper. They may not write anything in their answer booklets until told to do so by the invigilator.

London
School of Business
& Finance

shaping success in business and finance

The Essentials module papers all have a Section A containing a major case study question with all requirements totalling 50 marks relating to this case. Section B gives students a choice of two from three 25 mark questions.

Section A of each of the Options papers contains 50-70 compulsory marks from two questions, each attracting between 25 and 40 marks. Section B will offer a choice of two of three questions totalling 30-50 marks, with each question attracting between 15 and 25 marks.

The pass mark for all ACCA Qualification examination papers is 50%.

## Guide to Examination Assessment

ACCA reserves the right to examine anything contained within the study guide at any examination session. This includes knowledge, techniques, principles, theories, and concepts as specified.

For the financial accounting, audit and assurance, law and tax papers, except where indicated otherwise, ACCA will publish examinable documents once a year to indicate exactly what regulations and legislation could potentially be assessed within identified examination sessions.

For paper based examinations regulation issued or legislation passed on or before 30th September annually, will be assessed from June 1st of the following year to May 31st of the year after. Therefore, paper based examinations in June 2009, December 2009 (and March 2010 where applicable) will be assessed on regulations issued and legislation passed on or before 30 September 2008.

Regulation issued or legislation passed in accordance with the above dates may be examinable even if the effective date is in the future.

The term issued or passed relates to when regulation or legislation has been formally approved. The term effective relates to when regulation or legislation must be applied to an entity's transactions and business practices.

The study guide offers more detailed guidance on the depth and level at which the examinable documents will be examined. The study guide should therefore be read in conjunction with the examinable documents list.

## Relational Diagram of Paper with Other Papers

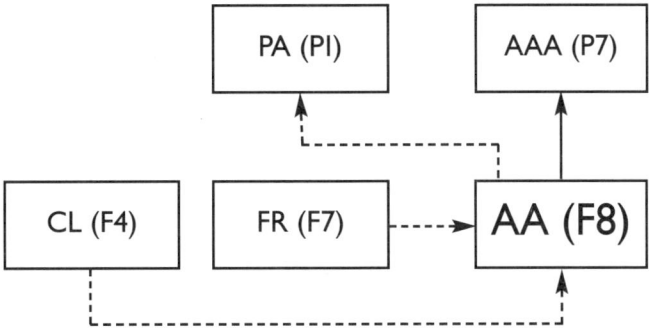

## Overall Aim of the Syllabus

To develop knowledge and understanding of the process of carrying out the assurance engagement and its application in the context of the professional regulatory framework.

## Main Capabilities

On successful completion of this paper candidates should be able to:

A  Explain the nature, purpose and scope of assurance engagements including the role of the external audit and its regulatory and ethical framework;

B  Explain the nature of internal audit and describe its role as part of overall performance management and its relationship with the external audit;

C  Demonstrate how the auditor obtains an understanding of the entity and its environment, assesses the risk of material misstatement (whether arising from fraud or other irregularities) and plans an audit of financial statements;

D  Describe and evaluate information systems and internal controls to identify and communicate control risks and their potential consequences, making appropriate recommendations;

E  Identify and describe the work and evidence required to meet the objectives of audit engagements and the application of the International Standards on Auditing;

F  Evaluate findings and modify the audit plan as necessary;

G  Explain how the conclusions from audit work are reflected in different types of audit report, explain the elements of each type of report.

## Relational Diagram of the Main Sections

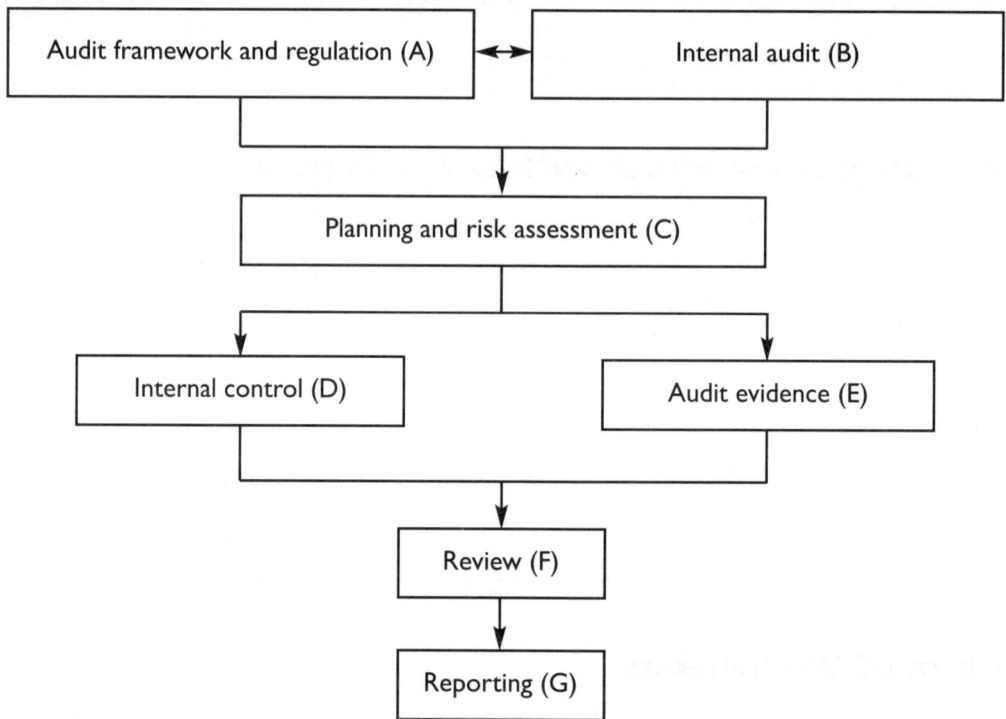

## Syllabus Rationale

The syllabus for Audit and Assurance is essentially divided into seven areas. The syllabus starts with the nature, purpose and scope of assurance engagements, including the statutory audit, its regulatory environment, and introduces
professional ethics relating to audit and assurance. It then leads into internal audit including the scope of internal audit as well as the differences between internal audit and external audit. The syllabus then covers a range of areas relating to an audit of financial statements. These include planning and risk assessment, evaluating internal controls, audit evidence, and a review of the financial statements. The final section then deals with reporting, including statutory

audit reports, management reports, and internal audit reports.

# Detailed Syllabus

A.    AUDIT FRAMEWORK AND REGULATION

    1.   The concept of audit and other assurance engagements

    2.   Statutory audits

    3.   The regulatory environment and corporate governance

    4.   Professional ethics and ACCA's Code of Ethics and Conduct

B.    INTERNAL AUDIT

    1.   Internal audit and corporate governance

    2.   Differences between external and internal audit

    3.   The scope of the internal audit function

    4.   Outsourcing the internal audit department

    5.   Internal audit assignments

C.    PLANNING AND RISK ASSESSMENT

    1.   Objective and general principles

    2.   Understanding the entity and knowledge of the business

    3.   Assessing the risks of material misstatement and fraud

    4.   Analytical procedures

    5.   Planning an audit

    6.   Audit documentation

    7.   The work of others

D.    INTERNAL CONTROL

    1.   Internal control systems

    2.   The use of internal control systems by auditors

    3.   Transaction cycles

    4.   Tests of control

    5.   The evaluation of internal control components

    6.   Communication on internal control

E.    AUDIT EVIDENCE

    1.   The use of assertions by auditors

    2.   Audit procedures

    3.   The audit of specific items

    4.   Audit sampling and other means of testing

    5.   Computer-assisted audit techniques

    6.   Not-for-profit organisations

F.    REVIEW

    1.   Subsequent events

    2.   Going concern

    3.   Management representations

    4.   Audit finalisation and the final review

G.    REPORTING

    1.   Audit reports

    2.   Reports to management

3.   Internal audit reports

## Approach to Examining the Syllabus

The syllabus is assessed by a three-hour paper-based examination, consisting of five compulsory questions. The bulk of the questions will be discursive but some questions involving computational elements will be set from time to time.

The questions will cover all areas of the syllabus.

Question 1 will be a scenario based question worth 30 marks. Question 2 will be a knowledge based question worth 10 marks. Questions 3, 4 and 5 will be worth 20 marks each.

# STUDY GUIDE

# A    Audit Framework and Regulation

1.    THE CONCEPT OF AUDIT AND OTHER ASSURANCE ENGAGEMENTS

a)    Identify and describe the objective and general principles of external audit engagements. [2]

b)    Explain the nature and development of audit and other assurance engagements. [1]

c)    Discuss the concepts of accountability, stewardship and agency. [2]

d)    Discuss the concepts of materiality, true and fair presentation and reasonable assurance. [2]

e)    Explain reporting as a means of communication to different stakeholders. [1]

f)    Explain the level of assurance provided by audit and other review assignments. [1]

2.    STATUTORY AUDITS

a)    Describe the regulatory environment within which statutory audits take place. [1]

b)    Discuss the reasons and mechanisms for the regulation of auditors. [2]

c)    Explain the statutory regulations governing the appointment, removal and resignation of auditors. [1]

d)    Discuss the types of opinion provided in statutory audits. [2]

e)    State the objectives and principle activities of statutory audit and assess its value (e.g. in assisting management to reduce risk and improve performance). [1]

f)    Describe the limitations of statutory audits. [1]

3.    THE REGULATORY ENVIRONMENT AND CORPORATE GOVERNANCE

a)    Explain the development and status of International Standards on Auditing. [1]

b)    Explain the relationship between International Standards on Auditing and National Standards. [1]

c)    Discuss the objective, relevance and importance of corporate governance. [2]

d)    Discuss the need for auditors to communicate with those charged with governance. [2]

e)    Discuss the provisions of international codes of corporate governance (such as the Organization for Economic Cooperation and Development) that are most relevant to auditors. [2]

f)    Describe good corporate governance requirements relating to directors' responsibilities (e.g. for risk management

and internal control) and the reporting responsibilities of auditors. [1]

g) Analyse the structure and roles of audit committees and discuss their drawbacks and limitations. [2]

h) Explain the importance of internal control and risk management. [1]

i) Compare the responsibilities of management and auditors for the design and operation of systems and controls. [2]

4. PROFESSIONAL ETHICS AND ACCA'S CODE OF ETHICS AND CONDUCT

a) Define and apply the fundamental principles of professional ethics of integrity, objectivity, professional competence and due care, confidentiality and professional behaviour. [2]

b) Define and apply the conceptual framework. [2]

c) Discuss the sources of, and enforcement mechanisms associated with, ACCA's Code of Ethics and Conduct. [2]

d) Discuss the requirements of professional ethics and other requirements in relation to the acceptance of new audit engagements. [2]

e) Discuss the process by which an auditor obtains an audit engagement. [2]

f) Explain the importance of engagement letters and state their contents. [1]

# B    Internal Audit

1. INTERNAL AUDIT AND CORPORATE GOVERNANCE

a) Discuss the factors to be taken into account when assessing the need for internal audit. [2]

b) Discuss the elements of best practice in the structure and operations of internal audit with reference to appropriate international codes of corporate governance. [2]

2. DIFFERENCES BETWEEN EXTERNAL AND INTERNAL AUDIT

a) Compare and contrast the role of external and internal audit regarding audit planning and the collection of audit evidence. [2]

b) Compare and contrast the types of report provided by internal and external audit. [2]

3. THE SCOPE OF THE INTERNAL AUDIT FUNCTION

a) Discuss the scope of internal audit and the limitations of the internal audit function. [2]

b) Explain the types of audit report provided in internal audit assignments. [1]

c) Discuss the responsibilities of internal and external auditors for the prevention and detection of fraud and error. [2]

4. OUTSOURCING THE INTERNAL AUDIT DEPARTMENT

a) Explain the advantages and disadvantages of outsourcing internal audit. [1]

5. INTERNAL AUDIT ASSIGNMENTS

a) Discuss the nature and purpose of internal audit assignments including value for money, IT, best value and financial. [2]

b) Discuss the nature and purpose of operational internal audit assignments including procurement, marketing, treasury and human resources management. [2]

# C Planning and Risk Assessment

1. OBJECTIVE AND GENERAL PRINCIPLES

a) Identify and describe the need to plan and perform audits with an attitude of professional scepticism. [2]

b) Identify and describe engagement risks affecting the audit of an entity. [1]

c) Explain the components of audit risk. [1]

d) Compare and contrast risk-based, procedural and other approaches to audit work. [2]

e) Discuss the importance of risk analysis. [2]

f) Describe the use of information technology in risk analysis. [1]

2. UNDERSTANDING THE ENTITY AND KNOWLEDGE OF THE BUSINESS

a) Explain how auditors obtain an initial understanding of the entity and knowledge of its business environment. [2]

3. ASSESSING THE RISKS OF MATERIAL MISSTATEMENT AND FRAUD

a) Define and explain the concepts of materiality and tolerable error. [2]

b) Compute indicative materiality levels from financial information. [2]

c) Discuss the effect of fraud and misstatements on the audit strategy and extent of audit work. [2]

4. ANALYTICAL PROCEDURES

a) Describe and explain the nature and purpose of analytical procedures in planning. [2]

b) Compute and interpret key ratios used in analytical procedures. [2]

5. PLANNING AN AUDIT

a) Identify and explain the need for planning an audit. [2]

b) Identify and describe the contents of the overall audit strategy and audit plan. [2]

c) Explain and describe the relationship between the overall audit strategy and the audit plan. [2]

d) Develop and document an audit plan. [2]

e) Explain the difference between interim and final audit. [1]

6. AUDIT DOCUMENTATION

a) Explain the need for and the importance of audit documentation. [1]

b) Describe and prepare working papers and supporting documentation .[2]

c) Explain the procedures to ensure safe custody and retention of working papers. [1]

7. THE WORK OF OTHERS

a) Discuss the extent to which auditors are able to rely on the work of experts. [2]

b) Discuss the extent to which external auditors are able to rely on the work of internal audit. [2]

London
School of Business
& Finance
shaping success in business and finance

c)   Discuss the audit considerations relating to entities using service organisations. [2]

d)   Discuss why auditors rely on the work of others. [2]

e)   Explain the extent to which reference to the work of others can be made in audit reports. [1]

# D   Internal Control

The following transaction cycles and account balances are relevant to this capability:

- revenue;
- purchases;
- inventory;
- revenue and capital expenditure;
- payroll;
- bank and cash.

1.   INTERNAL CONTROL SYSTEMS

a)   Explain why an auditor needs to obtain an understanding of internal control activities relevant to the audit. [1]

b)   Describe and explain the key components of an internal control system. [1]

c)   Identify and describe the important elements of internal control including the control environment and management control activities. [1]

d)   Discuss the difference between tests of control and substantive procedures. [2]

2.   THE USE OF INTERNAL CONTROL SYSTEMS BY AUDITORS

a)   Explain the importance of internal control to auditors. [1]

b)   Explain how auditors identify weaknesses in internal control systems and how those weaknesses limit the extent of auditors' reliance on those systems. [2]

3.   TRANSACTION CYCLES

a)   Explain, analyse and provide examples of internal control procedures and control activities. [2]

b)   Provide examples of computer system controls. [2]

4.   TESTS OF CONTROL

a)   Explain and tabulate tests of control suitable for inclusion in audit working papers. [2]

b)   List examples of application controls and general IT controls. [2]

5.   THE EVALUATION OF INTERNAL CONTROL COMPONENTS

a)   Analyse the limitations of internal control components in the context of fraud and error. [2]

b)   Explain the need to modify the audit strategy and audit plan following the results of tests of control. [1]

c)   Identify and explain management's risk assessment process with reference to internal control components. [1]

6.   COMMUNICATION ON INTERNAL CONTROL

a)   Discuss, and provide examples of, how the reporting of internal control weaknesses and recommendations to overcome those weaknesses are provided to management. [2]

# E    Audit Evidence

1.    THE USE OF ASSERTIONS BY AUDITORS

a)    Explain the assertions contained in the financial statements. [2]

b)    Explain the principles and objectives of transaction testing, account balance testing and disclosure testing. [1]

c)    Explain the use of assertions in obtaining audit evidence. [2]

2.    AUDIT PROCEDURES

a)    Discuss the sources and relative merits of the different types of evidence available. [2]

b)    Discuss and provide examples of how analytical procedures are used as substantive procedures. [2]

c)    Discuss the problems associated with the audit and review of accounting estimates. [2]

d)    Describe why smaller entities may have different control environments and describe the types of evidence likely to be available in smaller entities. [1]

e)    Discuss the quality of evidence obtained. [2]

3.    THE AUDIT OF SPECIFIC ITEMS

For each of the account balances stated in this sub-capability:
- explain the purpose of substantive procedures in relation to financial statement assertions;
- explain the substantive procedures used in auditing each balance; and
- tabulate those substantive procedures in a work program.

a)    Receivables: [2]

i)   direct confirmation of accounts receivable;

ii)  other evidence in relation to receivables and prepayments; and

iii) the related income statement entries.

b)    Inventory: [2]

i)   inventory counting procedures in relation to year end and continuous inventory systems;

ii)  cut-off;

iii) auditor's attendance at inventory counting;

iv) direct confirmation of inventory held by third parties;

v)  other evidence in relation to inventory.

c)    Payables and accruals: [2]

i)   supplier statement reconciliations and direct confirmation of accounts payable;

ii)  obtain evidence in relation to payables and accruals; and

iii) the related income statement entries.

London
School of Business
& Finance

shaping success in business and finance

d) Bank and cash: [2]

    i) bank confirmation reports used in obtaining evidence in relation to bank and cash;

    ii) other evidence in relation to bank and cash;

    iii) the related income statement entries.

e) Tangible non-current assets and long-term liabilities: [2]

    i) evidence in relation to non-current assets;

    ii) non-current liabilities;

    iii) the related income statement entries.

4. AUDIT SAMPLING AND OTHER MEANS OF TESTING

a) Define audit sampling and explain the need for sampling. [1]

b) Identify and discuss the differences between statistical and non-statistical sampling. [2]

c) Discuss, and provide relevant examples of, the application of the basic principles of statistical sampling and other selective testing procedures. [2]

d) Discuss the results of statistical sampling, including consideration of whether additional testing is required. [2]

5. COMPUTER-ASSISTED AUDIT TECHNIQUES

a) Explain the use of computer-assisted audit techniques in the context of an audit. [1]

b) Discuss and provide relevant examples of the use of test data and audit software for the transaction cycles and balances mentioned in sub-capability three. [2]

c) Discuss the use of computers in relation to the administration of the audit. [2]

6. NOT-FOR-PROFIT ORGANISATIONS

a) Apply audit techniques to small not-for-profit organisations. [2]

b) Explain how the audit of small not-for-profit organisations differs from the audit of for profit organisations. [1]

# F Review

1. SUBSEQUENT EVENTS

a) Explain the purpose of a subsequent events review. [1]

b) Discuss the procedures to be undertaken in performing a subsequent events review. [2]

2. GOING CONCERN

a) Define and discuss the significance of the concept of 'going concern'. [2]

b) Explain the importance of and the need for going concern reviews. [2]

c) Explain the respective responsibilities of auditors and management regarding going concern. [1]

d) Discuss the procedures to be applied in performing going concern reviews. [2]

e) Discuss the disclosure requirements in relation to going concern issues. [2]

f) Discuss the reporting implications of the findings of going concern reviews. [2]

3. MANAGEMENT REPRESENTATIONS

a) Explain the purpose of and procedure for obtaining management representations. [2]

b) Discuss the quality and reliability of management representations as audit evidence. [2]

c) Discuss the circumstances where management representations are necessary and the matters on which representations are commonly obtained. [2]

4. AUDIT FINALISATION AND THE FINAL REVIEW

a) Discuss the importance of the overall review of evidence obtained. [2]

b) Explain the significance of unadjusted differences. [1]

# G Reporting

1. AUDIT REPORTS

a) Describe and analyse the format and content of unmodified audit reports. [2]

b) Describe and analyse the format and content of modified audit reports. [2]

2. REPORTS TO MANAGEMENT

a) Identify and analyse internal control and system weaknesses and their potential effects and make appropriate recommendations to management. [2]

3. INTERNAL AUDIT REPORTS

a) Describe and explain the format and content of internal audit review reports and other reports dealing with the enhancement of performance. [1]

b) Explain the process for producing an internal audit report. [1]

# F8

## Pilot Paper

Please note that the Pilot Paper is the original ACCA document and is for guidance only. It has not been updated for any subsequent changes in laws and regulations, so some technical details may have changed since the original Pilot Paper was issued. For up-to-date exam questions and answers, please see the relevant Revision Kit.

London
School of Business
& Finance

shaping success in business and finance

Fundamentals Pilot Paper    Skills module

# Audit and Assurance
# (INT and UK)

**Time allowed**

Reading and planning:        15 minutes
Writing:                     3 hours

ALL FIVE questions are compulsory and MUST be attempted.

**Do NOT open this paper until instructed by the supervisor.**

**During reading and planning time only the question paper may be annotated. You must NOT write in your answer booklet until instructed by the supervisor.**

**This question paper must not be removed from the examination hall.**

**The Association of Chartered Certified Accountants**

# ALL FIVE questions are compulsory and MUST be attempted

1. Westra Co assembles mobile telephones in a large factory. Each telephone contains up to 100 different parts, with each part being obtained from one of 50 authorised suppliers.

Like many companies, Westra's accounting systems are partly manual and partly computerised. In overview the systems include:

(i) Design software;

(ii) A computerised database of suppliers (bespoke system written in-house at Westra);

(iii) A manual system for recording goods inwards and transferring information to the accounts department;

(iv) A computerised payables ledger maintained in the accounts department (purchased off-the-shelf and used with no program amendments);

(v) Online payment to suppliers, also in the accounts department;

(vi) A computerised general ledger which is updated by the payables ledger.

Mobile telephones are assembled in batches of 10,000 to 50,000 telephones. When a batch is scheduled for production, a list of parts is produced by the design software and sent, electronically, to the ordering department. Staff in the ordering department use this list to place orders with authorised suppliers. Orders can only be sent to suppliers on the suppliers' database. Orders are sent using electronic data interchange (EDI) and confirmed by each supplier using the same system. The list of parts and orders are retained on the computer in an 'orders placed' file, which is kept in date sequence.

Parts are delivered to the goods inwards department at Westra. All deliveries are checked against the orders placed file before being accepted. A hand-written pre-numbered goods received note (GRN) is raised in the goods inwards department showing details of the goods received with a cross-reference to the date of the order. The top copy of the GRN is sent to the accounts department and the second copy retained in the goods inwards department. The orders placed file is updated with the GRN number to show that the parts have been received.

Paper invoices are sent by all suppliers following dispatch of goods. Invoices are sent to the accounts department, where they are stamped with a unique ascending number. Invoice details are matched to the GRN, which is then attached to the invoice. Invoice details are then entered into the computerised payables ledger. The invoice is signed by the accounts clerk to confirm entry into the payables ledger. Invoices are then retained in a temporary file in number order while awaiting payment.

After 30 days, the payables ledger automatically generates a computerised list of payments to be made, which is sent electronically to the chief accountant. The chief accountant compares this list to the invoices, signs each invoice to indicate approval for payment, and then forwards the electronic payments list to the accounts assistant. The assistant uses online banking to pay the suppliers. The electronic payments list is filed in month order on the computer.

**Required:**

(a) **List the substantive audit procedures you should perform to confirm the assertions of completeness, occurrence and cut-off for purchases in the financial statements of Westra Co. For each procedure, explain the purpose of that procedure.**
(12 Marks)

(b) **List the audit procedures you should perform on the trade payables balance in Westra Co's financial statements. For each procedure, explain the purpose of that procedure.** (8 Marks)

(c) **Describe the control procedures that should be in place over the standing data on the trade payables master file in Westra Co's computer system.** (5 Marks)

(d) **Discuss the extent to which computer-assisted audit techniques might be used in your audit of purchases and payables at Westra Co.** (5 Marks)

**(30 marks)**

2. **(a)** ISA 210 Terms of Audit Engagements explains the content and use of engagement letters.

   **Required:**

   **State six items that could be included in an engagement letter.** (3 marks)

   **(b)** ISA 500 Audit Evidence explains types of audit evidence that the auditor can obtain.

   **Required:**

   **State, and briefly explain, four types of audit evidence that can be obtained by the auditor.** (4 marks)

   **(c)** ISA 700 The Independent Auditor's Report on a Complete Set of General Purpose Financial Statements explains the form and content of audit reports.

   **Required:**

   **State three ways in which an auditor's report may be modified and briefly explain the use of each modification.** (3 marks)

   **(10 marks)**

3. You are the audit manager in the audit firm of Dark & Co. One of your audit clients is NorthCee Co, a company specialising in the manufacture and supply of sporting equipment. NorthCee have been an audit client for five years and you have been audit manager for the past three years while the audit partner has remained unchanged.

   You are now planning the audit for the year ending 31 December 2007. Following an initial meeting with the directors of NorthCee, you have obtained the following information.

   (i) NorthCee is attempting to obtain a listing on a recognised stock exchange. The directors have established an audit committee, as required by corporate governance regulations, although no further action has been taken in this respect. Information on the listing is not yet public knowledge.

   (ii) You have been asked to continue to prepare the company's financial statements as in previous years.

   (iii) As the company's auditors, NorthCee would like you and the audit partner to attend an evening reception in a hotel, where NorthCee will present their listing arrangements to banks and existing major shareholders.

   (iv) NorthCee has indicated that the fee for taxation services rendered in the year to 31 December 2005 will be paid as soon as the taxation authorities have agreed the company's taxation liability. You have been advising NorthCee regarding the legality of certain items as 'allowable' for taxation purposes and the taxation authority is disputing these items.

   Finally, you have just inherited about 5% of NorthCee's share capital as an inheritance on the death of a distant relative.

   **Required:**

   **(a)** **Identify, and explain the relevance of, any factors which may threaten the independence of Dark & Co's audit of NorthCee Co's financial statements for the year ending 31 December 2007. Briefly explain how each threat should be managed.** (10 Marks)

   **(b)** **Explain the actions that the board of directors of NorthCee Co must take in order to meet corporate governance requirements for the listing of NorthCee Co.** (6 Marks)

   **(c)** **Explain why your audit firm will need to communicate with NorthCee Co's audit committee for this and future audits.** (4 Marks)

   **(20 Marks)**

4.  SouthLea Co is a construction company (building houses, offices and hotels) employing a large number of workers on various construction sites. The internal audit department of SouthLea Co is currently reviewing cash wages systems within the company.

The following information is available concerning the wages systems:

(i)     Hours worked are recorded using a clocking in/out system. On arriving for work and at the end of each day's work, each worker enters their unique employee number on a keypad.

(ii)    Workers on each site are controlled by a foreman. The foreman has a record of all employee numbers and can issue temporary numbers for new employees.

(iii)   Any overtime is calculated by the computerised wages system and added to the standard pay.

(iv)    The two staff in the wages department make amendments to the computerised wages system in respect of employee holidays and illness, as well as setting up and maintaining all employee records.

(v)     The computerised wages system calculates deductions from gross pay, such as employee taxes, and net pay. Finally a list of net cash payments for each employee is produced.

(vi)    Cash is delivered to the wages office by secure courier.

(vii)   The two staff place cash into wages packets for each employee along with a handwritten note of gross pay, deductions and net pay. The packets are given to the foreman for distribution to the individual employees.

**Required:**

**(a) (i) Identify and explain weaknesses in SouthLea Co's system of internal control over the wages system that could lead to mis-statements in the financial statements.**

**(ii) For each weakness, suggest an internal control to overcome that weakness.**
(8 Marks)

**(b) Compare the responsibilities of the external and internal auditors to detect fraud.**
(6 Marks)

The computer system in the wages department needs to be replaced. The replacement will be carried out under the control of a specialist external consultant.

**Required:**

**(c) Explain the factors that should be taken into consideration when appointing an external consultant.** (6 Marks)

**(20 Marks)**

5.  EastVale Co manufactures a range of dairy products (for example, milk, yoghurt and cheese) in one factory. Products are stored in a nearby warehouse (which is rented by EastVale) before being sold to 350 supermarkets located within 200 kilometres of EastVale's factory. The products are perishable with an average shelf life of eight days. EastVale's financial statements year end is 31 July.

It is four months since the year end at your audit client of EastVale and the annual audit of EastVale is almost complete, but the auditor's report has not been signed.

The following events have just come to your attention. Both events occurred in late November.

(a)  A fire in the warehouse rented by the company has destroyed 60% of the inventory held for resale.

(b)  A batch of cheese produced by EastVale was found to contain some chemical impurities. Over 300 consumers have complained about food poisoning after eating the cheese. 115 supermarkets have stopped purchasing EastVale's products and another 85 are considering whether to stop purchasing from EastVale. Lawyers acting on behalf of the consumers are now presenting a substantial claim for damages against EastVale.

**Required:**

**In respect of EACH of the events at EastVale Co mentioned above:**

**(i)   Describe the additional audit procedures you will carry out.** (8 Marks)

**(ii)  State, with reasons, whether or not the financial statements for the year end require amendment.** (6 Marks)

**(iii) Discuss whether or not the audit report should be modified.** (6 Marks)

**Note: The total marks will be split equally between each event.**

**(20 Marks)**

End of Question Paper

London
School of Business
& Finance
shaping success in business and finance

# Answers

Tutorial note: some answers are longer than could be expected from candidates sitting this examination. The answers may also include more points than would be necessary to obtain full marks in the examination. This is to provide examples of valid points that could be made.

## I. Audit Procedures

### (a) Audit Procedures – Purchases

| AUDIT PROCEDURE | REASON FOR PROCEDURE |
|---|---|
| Obtain a sample of list of parts documents from the computer. Trace individual parts to the goods received note (GRN). | Checks the completeness of recording of liabilities. |
| For entries in the list of parts where no GRN number has been entered, enquire with goods inwards staff why there is no GRN. Document reasons obtained. | Checks that goods have not been received but details not recorded. Possible cut-off error where goods have been received but GRN not raised. |
| Obtain a sample of GRNs. Agree details to the list of parts document on the computer. | Ensures that the parts received had been ordered by Westra, giving evidence for the occurrence assertion. |
| For a sample of GRNs from the goods inwards department, trace to the invoice held in the accounts department. | Ensures the completeness of recording of liabilities. GRNs with no matching invoice indicate a liability has been incurred. Unmatched GRNs should be included in the payables accrual.<br>Note this test will be difficult because there is no cross reference maintained of the GRN to the invoice. |
| Review file of unmatched GRNs, investigate reasons for any old (more than one week) items. | Ensures the completeness of recording of liabilities. Unmatched items prior to the year end should be included in the payables accrual. |
| Obtain a sample of paid invoices. Ensure that the GRN is attached. | Confirms that the invoice should be included in the payables ledger, meeting the completeness assertion. |
| For the sample of invoices, check details into the computerised payables ledger, ensuring the correct account has been updated and the invoice amount is accurate. | Confirms the completeness of recording of payables invoices in the ledger. |
| Obtain the unmatched invoices file. Investigate old items obtaining reason for GRN not being received/ invoice not being processed. | Unmatched items at the year end could indicate unrecorded liabilities. Ensure included in the payables accrual if the invoice not being processed, goods had been received pre year end. |
| For a sample of entries from the payables ledger, agree details back to the purchase invoice. | Ensures that the liability does belong to Westra, meeting the occurrence assertion. |
| For the sample of entries on the payables ledger, agree to the electronic payments list confirming that the supplier name and amount is correct. | Ensures that the liability has been properly discharged by Westra and that the payments list is therefore complete. |
| For a sample of entries on each electronic payments list, agree details to the purchase invoice. | Ensures that the payment has been made for a liability incurred by Westra, meeting the occurrence assertion. |
| For the sample of entries in the electronic payments list, agree details to the bank statement. | Shows that the payment was actually made to that supplier. |

**(a) Audit Procedures – purchases continued**

| AUDIT PROCEDURE | REASON FOR PROCEDURE |
|---|---|
| Obtain the bank statements. Trace a sample of payments to the electronic payments list. | Confirms that the payment made does relate to Westra, confirming the occurrence assertion. |
| For a sample of GRNs in the week pre and post year end, trace to the supporting invoice and entry in the payables ledger, ensuring recorded in the correct accounting year. | Confirms the accuracy of cut-off in the financial statements. |

Tutorial note: this answer follows the structure of the scenario provided in the question. An alternative and valid format would be to use the assertions as main headings and to make points under each heading.

**(b) Audit Procedures – payables**

| AUDIT PROCEDURE | REASON FOR PROCEDURE |
|---|---|
| Obtain a list of payables balances from the computerised payables ledger as at Westra's year end. Cost the list. | To ensure that the list is accurate and that the total is represented by the individual balances (completeness assertion). |
| Agree the total of payables to the general ledger and financial statements. | To confirm that the total has been accurately recorded and financial statements. that the balance in the financial statements is represented by valid payables (occurrence assertion). |
| Perform analytical procedures on the list of payables. Determine reasons for any unusual changes in the total balance or individual payables in the list. | Provides initial indication of the accuracy and completeness of the list of payables. |
| For a sample of payables on the list, agree to supplier statements at the year end. | Confirms that the payables balance is due from Westra meeting the occurrence assertion. |
| Reconcile supplier statement balances to the payables ledger. | Ensures that the liabilities exist and belong to Westra at the year end. |
| For invoices on the statements not in the ledger, agree to invoices entered after the year end. Check the date of goods receipt per the GRN attached to the invoice. Where goods received pre-year end agree invoice to the payables accrual. | Ensures that all liabilities were recorded at the year end, meeting the completeness and cut-off assertions. |
| For payments not included in the supplier statements, agree to the next month end statement ensuring that the payment has been recorded. | Ensures that payments have been made to the correct supplier. |
| Review the payables ledger for old unpaid invoices. Enquire of the chief accountant the reason for non-payment. | Non-payment may be indicative of goods being returned for credit indicating that the payables figure may be overstated. Alternatively, taking additional credit from payables may be a 'going concern' indicator. |
| Review credit notes received post year end ensuring that where they relate to pre-year end purchases that the payables accrual has been reduced. | Ensures that payables are not over-stated at the year end. Large credit notes may also be an indication of overstating payables deliberately to reduce profit. |
| Ensure that payables have been included in the financial statements under the heading of current liabilities. | Confirm the correct classification of payables in the financial statements. |

### (c) Controls over Standing Data

Controls include:

- Any amendment (addition, amendment or deletion) to the payables ledger should be authorised by a responsible official; for example, the chief accountant.
- Authorisation can be by a form signed manually by the chief accountant having a restricted access password to amend the standing data.
- The computer should reject deletion of a supplier account where there is an outstanding balance (debit or credit).
- A record of amendments made to the payables ledger should be maintained within the ledger and reviewed on a regular basis by the chief accountant to ensure that the changes are bona fide.
- The chief accountant should review the list of suppliers on a regular basis (perhaps every four to six months) and delete those which are no longer used.
- A comparison should be made regularly (perhaps every month) between the authorised list of suppliers on the computerised list of suppliers and the payables ledger. Any new supplier on the list of suppliers should be added to the payables ledger in preparation for payment.
- A review of the computer control log regarding access to the payables standing data should be made on a regular basis and any unauthorised access identified and changes made under that access identified and if necessary reversed.
- A list of suppliers should be printed out occasionally (about every three months) and kept in a secure location in the chief accountant's office. The chief accountant should then compare this list with the computerised list in three months time and account for any unauthorised additions.

### (d) Use of Computer-Assisted Audit Techniques

Audit software may be used to identify old/obsolete balances in some of Westra's systems, for example outstanding deliveries and payments not being made to suppliers. However, the usefulness of the testing is limited and it is possible that the computer system already provides similar controls.

Test data input by the auditor would be useful in checking the online payments system, perhaps by setting up some "dummy" accounts and ensuring that payments are sent to the correct suppliers. Other controls over payments such as access controls are more likely to be tested manually by the auditor.

Use of Computer-Assisted Audit Techniques (CAATs) may be limited in Westra due to the lack of integration of computer systems. For example, the suppliers' database is not connected to the payables ledger, limiting the use of test data to check transactions all the way through the purchases/payables system.

There is no indication provided in the scenario regarding the extent and effectiveness of computer controls. Controls would have to be identified and assessed for reliability prior to reliance being placed.

Given that some of Westra's systems are bespoke, then it may not be cost effective to use CAATs given the time required to write specific test data or program audit software to use Westra's data.

Use of CAATs in the suppliers' database may not be effective given that the database does not input directly into any financial accounting system. Testing GRNs to purchase invoice to ledgers, etc will provide greater assurance of the completeness and accuracy of purchases than testing the suppliers' database.

## 2. Engagement Letter

L

### (a) Contents of an Engagement Letter

- Objective of the audit of the financial statements.
- Management's responsibility for the financial statements.
- The scope of the audit with reference to appropriate legislation.
- The form of any report or other communication of the results of the engagement.
- The auditor may not discover all material errors.
- Provision of access to the auditor of all relevant books and records.
- Arrangements for planning the audit.
- Agreement of management to provide a representation letter.
- Request that the client confirms in writing the terms of engagement.
- Description of any letters or reports to be issued to the client.
- Basis of fee calculation and billing arrangements.

### (b) Types of Audit Evidence

- Inspection – examination of records or documents in whatever form, for example manual computerised, external or internal.
- Observation – looking at the processes or procedures being carried out by others.
- Inquiry – seeking information from knowledgeable persons, both financial or non-financial, either within or outside the entity being audited.
- Confirmation – the process of obtaining a representation of an existing condition from a third party, for example a receivables letter.
- Recalculation – checking the mathematical accuracy of documents or records.
- Reperformance – this is the auditor's independent execution of procedures or controls that were originally performed as part of the entity's internal control system.
- Analytical procedures – evaluation of financial information made by a study of plausible relationships among both financial and non-financial data.

### (c) Modification of Audit Reports

- Emphasis of matter paragraph. Used where the auditor wishes to draw attention to an important item in the financial statements.
- Qualification – limitation in scope. Used where the audit cannot obtain sufficient evidence regarding an item in the financial statements.
- Qualification – disagreement. Used where the auditor disagrees concerning the amount or disclosure of an item in the financial statements.

### 3.(a) Threats to Independence

ROTATION OF AUDIT PARTNER

NorthCee Co have had the same audit partner for the last five years. An audit partner's independence may be impaired where that position is retained for more than five years for a listed company. The reason being that the partner has become too close to the directors and staff in the firm and this may impair his judgement on the financial statements. However, NorthCee is currently not listed so this requirement does not apply.

As NorthCee is now being listed, Dark & Co should rotate the audit partner this year to avoid any familiarity threat. However, given that NorthCee was not a listed company up to this audit, this may imply that the partner could continue this year, but would be recommended to be rotated before the 2008 audit.

PREPARATION OF FINANCIAL STATEMENTS

Apparently Dark have been preparing NorthCee's financial statements as well as carrying out the audit in previous years. While this may not have been an independence issue in the past, it is likely to be now as in many jurisdictions auditors may not provide other services to their audit clients, especially listed client. Preparing financial statements as well as auditing them would provide Dark with a self-review threat, that is they may not see any errors, or want to report errors in material that they have previously prepared.

Dark should therefore decline from preparation of NorthCee's financial statements.

ATTENDANCE AT SOCIAL EVENT

Attending the social event with respect to the new listing may be inappropriate as Dark may be seen as supporting NorthCee in this venture. There is an advocacy threat to independence. Support for a client may imply that the audit firm are "too close" to that client and may therefore lose their independent view regarding the audit. There is also a familiarity threat.

Dark should therefore politely decline the dinner invitation, clearly stating their reasons.

UNPAID TAXATION FEE

The unpaid fee in respect of taxation services could be construed as a loan to the audit client. Audit firms should not make loans to or receive loans from audit clients. An outstanding loan will affect independence as closure of the loan may be seen as more important than providing an appropriate audit opinion.

Dark need to discuss the situation with NorthCee again, suggesting that a payment on account could be made to show that the whole fee will be paid. Alternatively, audit work on the 2007 financial statements can be delayed until the taxation fee is paid.

INHERITANCE

Under ACCA's Code of Ethics and Conduct, audit partners may not hold beneficial shares in a client company. This provision includes audit staff where they are involved in the audit. The independence issue is simply that the shareholder (the auditor in this case) may be more interested in the value of the shares than providing a "correct" opinion on the financial statements.

The shares should be disposed of as soon as possible. However, given the inside knowledge of the listing, disposal now, or delaying disposal a few days to obtain a better price may be considered "insider dealing". It may be better that the audit manager resigns from the audit immediately to limit any real or potential independence problems. Professional advice may be needed on when to sell the shares.

## (b) Meeting Corporate Governance Requirements

Currently, the only action that the directors appear to have taken is to establish an audit committee. Given that NorthCee is going to be listed on a recognised stock exchange, then there are other corporate governance requirements to be met. These requirements include:

- Ensuring that the chairman and the company chief executive officer (CEO) are different people.
- Appointing non-executive directors (NEDs) to the board of NorthCee. The number of NEDs should be the same as the number of executive directors less the chairman.
- Ensuring that at least one NED has relevant financial experience.
- Appointing the NEDs to the audit committee, remuneration committee and possibly an appointments committee. The chairman will also have a seat on these committees.
- Establishing an internal audit department to review NorthCee's internal control systems and make reports to the audit committee.
- Ensure that NorthCee has an appropriate system of internal control and that the directors recognise their responsibilities for establishing and maintaining this system.
- Establishing procedures to maintain contact with institutional shareholders and any other major shareholders. The evening reception for shareholders could become a regular event in this respect.
- Checking that the annual financial report contains information on corporate governance required by the stock exchange (eg a report on how directors monitor the internal control systems).

## (c) Communication with the Audit Committee

Under most systems of corporate governance, the external auditor's primary point of contact with a company is the audit committee. There are various reasons for this:

- Initially, to ensure that there is independence between the board of directors and the audit firm. The audit committee consists of non-executive directors (NEDs), who by definition are independent of the company and can therefore take an objective view of the audit report.
- The audit committee will have more time to review the audit report and other communications to the company from the auditor (eg management letters) than the board. The auditor should therefore benefit from their reports being reviewed carefully.
- The audit committee can ensure that any recommendations from the auditor are implemented. The audit committee has independent NEDs who can pressurise the board to taking action on auditor recommendations.
- The audit committee also has more time to review the effectiveness and efficiency of the work of the external auditor than the board. The committee can therefore make recommendations on the re-appointment of the auditor, or recommend a different firm if this would be appropriate.

## 4 (a)  Control Weaknesses and Recommendations

| CONTROL WEAKNESS | INTERNAL CONTROL RECOMMENDATION |
| --- | --- |
| Employees can be paid for work not done. There appears to be no check to ensure that hours recorded in the computer system actually relate to hours worked. | A record of hours worked by each employee should be printed from the computerised wages system and signed by the site foreman to confirm that the hours are accurate. |
| There is no check to ensure that each employee inputs his/her employee number. One employee could input two numbers hiding the fact that one employee is absent. | The computerised wages system should print a list of employees present per the computer system during the day and the foreman should then sign this list to confirm it is accurate. |
| Fake or dummy employees can be put onto the payroll. The foreman can set up employee records for workers who do not exist. As payment is made automatically from the record of hours worked. | The wages office should check the list of employees against personnel records of authorised employees. Any new employees should be verified in this way before payment is made. |
| The staff in the wages office could collude by setting up fake employee records in a similar way to the site foreman. | The list of employees on the payroll should be checked for accuracy by a person outside of the wages department, for example the personnel department or the chief accountant. The list of net payments should be signed by this person to show it is correct. |
| Gross pay inflated by wages department staff. The staff in the wages department could add extra hours to the records of some employees, and remove the net pay from the payment received from the courier prior to making up the pay packets. | The computerised payroll system should be programmed to produce a list of all amendments made to the payroll. This list should be reviewed by a responsible official outside of the wages department prior to wages being paid. |
| | Alternatively, the computerised payroll system should produce payslips for each employee showing the hours worked, gross and net pay etc. Employees should then check that the cash paid agrees to the net payment recorded on the payslip. |

## (b)  Fraud and External/Internal Audit

Guidance on the auditor's responsibility with respect to fraud can be found in ISA 240 *The Auditor's Responsibility to Consider Fraud in an Audit of Financial Statements*.

MAIN REASON FOR AUDIT WORK

The external auditor is primarily responsible for the audit opinion on the financial statements. The main focus of audit work is therefore to ensure that the financial statements show a true and fair view. The detection of fraud is therefore not the main focus of the external auditor's work.

The main focus of the work of the internal auditor is checking that the internal control systems in a company are working correctly. Part of that work may be to conduct a detailed review of systems to ensure that fraud is not taking place.

MATERIALITY

In reaching the audit opinion and performing audit work, the external auditor takes into account the concept of materiality. In other words, the external auditor is not responsible for checking all transactions. Audit procedures are planned to have a reasonable likelihood of identifying material fraud.

However, internal auditors may carry out a detailed review of transactions, effectively using a much lower materiality limit. It is more likely that internal auditors will detect fraud from their audit testing.

IDENTIFICATION OF FRAUD

In situations where the external auditor does detect fraud, then the auditor will need to consider the implications for the entire audit. In other words, the external auditor has a responsibility to extend testing into other areas because the risk of providing an incorrect audit opinion will have increased.

Where internal auditors detect fraud, they may extend testing into other areas. However, audit work is more likely to focus on determining the extent of fraud and ensuring similar fraud has not occurred in other locations.

## (c) Use of Expert

QUALIFICATION

The consultant should have a relevant qualification to show ability to undertake the work. In this case being a member of a relevant computer society or the Institute of Internal Auditors would be appropriate.

EXPERIENCE

The consultant should be able to show relevant experience from previous projects for example; upgrading or amending wages systems for other clients.

REFERENCES

Hopefully the consultant will be able to provide references from previous employers showing capability to undertake the work.

PROJECT MANAGEMENT SKILLS

The consultant should be able to display appropriate project management skills, as managing a team will be an important element of the systems change work.

ACCESS TO INFORMATION

The consultant will need access to important and sensitive information in SouthLea. The chief accountant must ensure that this information will be made available to third parties. The consultant will have to sign a confidentiality agreement.

ACCEPTANCE BY OTHER STAFF

Employing a consultant can be difficult as other internal audit staff may feel threatened or resentful that a consultant has been employed. The chief internal auditor must ensure that the reasons for employing the consultant are understood by members of the internal audit department.

## 5 (a) Fire at Warehouse

(i) AUDIT PROCEDURES

- Discuss the matter with the directors checking whether the company has sufficient inventory to continue trading in the short term.
- Enquire if the directors are satisfied that the company can continue to trade in the longer term. Ask the directors to sign an additional letter of representation to this effect.
- Obtain a schedule showing the inventory destroyed and if possible check this is reasonable given past production records and inventory valuations.
- Enquire that the insurers have been informed. Review correspondence from the insurers confirming the amount of the insurance claim.
- Consider whether or not EastVale can continue as a going concern, given the loss of inventory and potential damage to the company's reputation if customer orders cannot be fulfilled.

(ii) AMENDMENT TO FINANCIAL STATEMENTS

- Enquire as to whether the directors have considered whether the event needs disclosure in the financial statements. Disclosure is unlikely given that the inventory was not in existence at the year end and on the assumption that insurance is adequate to cover the loss.

- Amendment is not required as the fire did not affect any company property and the inventory would not have been in existence at the year end (inventory turn being very high).

### (iii) MODIFICATION OF AUDIT REPORT

- Consider modifying the audit report with an emphasis of matter paragraph to draw attention to the disclosure of the note on the fire in the financial statements.
- If the going concern status of EastVale is in doubt, then consider modifying the audit report with an emphasis of matter paragraph to this effect.
- If disclosure made by the directors is considered to be inadequate, then modify the audit report with an "except for" qualification.

## (b) Batch of Cheese

### (i) AUDIT PROCEDURES

- Discuss the matter with the directors, determining specifically whether there was any fault in the production process.
- Obtain a copy of the damages claim and again discuss with the directors the effect on EastVale and the possibility of success of the claim.
- Obtain independent legal advice on the claim from EastVale's lawyers. Attempt to determine the extent of damages that may have to be paid.
- Review any press reports about the contaminated cheese. Consider the impact on the reputation of EastVale and whether the company can continue as a going concern.
- Discuss the going concern issue with the directors. Obtain an additional letter of representation on the directors' opinion of the going concern status of EastVale.

### (ii) AMENDMENT TO FINANCIAL STATEMENTS

- The event should be disclosed in the financial statements in accordance with IAS 37 Provisions, Contingent Liabilities and Contingent Assets as it may have a significant impact on EastVale. Over two-thirds of EastVale's customers have either stopped purchasing products from the company or are considering taking this action.
- No adjustment is required for the event itself as it was not a condition at the balance sheet date.
- However, the event may require adjusting if company's reputation has been damaged and the amount of the legal claim is significant. In this situation the directors may decide that EastVale is no longer a going concern so the financial statements may have to be re-drafted on a break-up basis. This action complies with International Accounting Standard 8; the break-up basis is used where the directors have no realistic alternative but to liquidate the company.

### (iii) MODIFICATION OF AUDIT REPORT

Modification of the audit report depends on the director's actions above.

- If the financial statements are prepared on a breakup basis, and the auditor agrees with that assessment, then a modified report can be issued with an emphasis of matter paragraph drawing attention to the accounting basis used.
- However, if the financial statements are prepared on a going concern basis then the auditor should consider modifying the audit report with an emphasis of matter paragraph to draw attention to the disclosure of the note on the fire in the financial statements. This is providing that the auditor agrees that the going concern basis is appropriate.
- If the going concern status of EastVale is in doubt, then consider modifying the audit report with an emphasis of matter paragraph to this effect, drawing attention to disclosure made by the directors.
- If EastVale is not a going concern, and the financial statements have been prepared using this assumption, qualify the audit report with an adverse qualification stating that the company is not a going concern.

# Marking Scheme

**1 (a)  Audit Procedures – purchases** 12 marks. 1 for procedure and 1 for the reason. Limit to 0.5 mark in each category where stated briefly without full detail.

| AUDIT PROCEDURE | REASON FOR PROCEDURE | MARKS |
|---|---|---|
| Parts to GRN | Check completeness | |
| Parts with no GRN number | System error or cut-off error | |
| GRN to computer | Parts received were ordered – occurrence | |
| GRN agree to invoice | Completeness of recording | |
| Review unmatched GRN file | Completeness of recording of liabilities | |
| Paid invoice – GRN attached | Confirms invoice in PDB | |
| Invoice details to payables ledger | Completeness and accuracy of recording | |
| Review unmatched invoices file | Indicate understatement of liability (lack of completeness) | |
| Payables ledger to purchase invoice | Liability belongs to Westra | |
| Payables ledger to payments list | Liability properly discharged – payments complete | |
| Payment list entries to invoice | Payment made for bona fide liability | |
| Payments list to bank statement | Confirms payment to supplier | |
| Bank statement entry to payments list | Confirms payment relates to Westra | |
| GRN cut-off testing | Accuracy of cut-off | |

**Maximum marks**      **12**

**(b)  Audit Procedures – payables** 8 marks. 1 for procedure and 1 for the reason. Limit to 0.5 mark in each category where stated briefly without full detail.

| AUDIT PROCEDURE | REASON FOR PROCEDURE | MARKS |
|---|---|---|
| Obtain and cast list of payables | Ensure that the list is accurate | |
| Total of payables to the general ledger and financial statements | Confirm that the total has been accurately recorded | |
| Analytical procedures | Indicates problems with the accuracy and completeness of payables | |
| Agree payables to supplier statements | Confirm balance due from Westra | |
| Supplier statement reconciliation | Liabilities exist and belong to Westra | |
| Reconcile invoices | Confirms completeness and cut-off assertions | |
| Reconcile payments | Payment to correct supplier | |
| Review ledger old unpaid invoices | Credits OS or going concern indicator | |
| Date credit notes | Payables not overstated | |
| FS categorisation payables | Classification objective | |

**Maximum marks**      **8**

**(c)  Controls over Standing Data** 5 marks. 1 mark for explaining each control. 0.5 for poor/limited explanation.
Amendments authorised
How authorised (form or access control)
Reject deletion where outstanding balance
Keep record of amendments
Review list of suppliers – unauthorised amendments
Update supplier list on computer regularly
Review computer control log
Review list of suppliers – unauthorised additions
Other relevant points (each)

**Maximum marks**      **5**

MARKS

**(d)**     **Use of CAATs**                                                                    5

Review computer control log
Identify old/obsolete – computer may already do this
Test data – online payments system
Use of CAATs – limited – lack of computer system integration
Need to assess computer controls prior to use of CAATs
Not cost effective – bespoke systems
Limited use of CAATs in suppliers ledger
Other relevant points (each)

**Maximum marks**                                                                                5

**2      Engagement Letter**

**(a)   Contents of an Engagement Letter** 3 marks.  0.5 mark per point.

| | |
|---|---|
| Objective of the audit of the financial statements | 0.5 |
| Management's responsibility for the financial statements | 0.5 |
| The scope of the audit with reference to appropriate legislation | 0.5 |
| The form of any report or other communication of the results of the engagement | 0.5 |
| The auditor may not discover all material errors | 0.5 |
| Provision of access to the auditor of all relevant books and records | 0.5 |
| Arrangements for planning the audit | 0.5 |
| Agreement of management to provide a representation letter | 0.5 |
| Request that the client confirms in writing the terms of engagement | 0.5 |
| Description of any letters or reports to be issued to the client | 0.5 |
| Basis of fee calculation and billing arrangements | 0.5 |

**Maximum marks**                                                                                3

**(b)   Types of Audit Evidence** 4 marks: 0.5 only for stating the type and 0.5 for explanation.  Maximum 2 marks for simply providing a list of types of evidence.

| | |
|---|---|
| Inspection | 1 |
| Observation | 1 |
| Inquiry | 1 |
| Confirmation | 1 |
| Recalculation | 1 |
| Reperformance | 1 |
| Analytical procedures | 1 |

**Maximum marks**                                                                                4

**c)    Modification of Audit Reports** 3 marks.  0.5 for the type of report and 0.5 for explanation.

| | |
|---|---|
| Emphasis of matter paragraph | 1 |
| Qualification – limitation in scope | 1 |
| Qualification – disagreement | 1 |

**Maximum marks**                                                                                3

MARKS

**3 (a)** **Threats to Independance** 10 marks. 0.5 for identifying risk area, 1 for explanation of risk and 1 for stating how to resolve. Maximum 2.5 for each area.

Rotation of audit partner
Preparation of financial statements
Attendance at social event
Unpaid taxation fee
Inheritance
Other relevant points (each)

**Maximum marks** | 10

**(b)** **Meeting Corporate Governance Requirements** 6 marks. 1 mark for each point.

Chief executive officer (CEO)/chairman split
Appoint NED
NED with financial experience
NEDs to sub-committees of board
Internal audit
Internal control system
Contact institutional shareholders
Financial report information
Other relevant points (each)

**Maximum marks** | 6

**(c)** **Communication with Audit Committee** 4 marks. 1 mark for each point.

| | |
|---|---|
| Independence from board | 1 |
| Time to review audit work | 1 |
| Check auditor recommendations implemented | 1 |
| Review work of internal auditor (efficiency, etc.) | 1 |
| Other relevant points (each) | 1 |

**Maximum marks** | 4

**4 (a)** **Control weaknesses and recommendations** 8 marks. 1 for explanation of weakness and 1 for internal control recommendation. Maximum 2 per weakness/recommendation.

| CONTROL WEAKNESS | RECOMMENDATION | MARKS |
|---|---|---|
| Employees can be paid for work not done. | | |
| No check on hours actually worked | Authorise hours worked on computer | |
| Fraudulent input employee number | Reconcile computer to actual employees | |
| Fake or dummy employees can be put onto the payroll. | | |
| Foreman setup | Check employees against personnel records | |
| Wages office staff setup | List of employees reviewed for accuracy | |
| Gross pay inflated by wages department staff. | | |
| Add extra hours work done | List amendments to payroll produced | |
| Other valid points | | |

**Maximum marks** | 8

London
School of Business
& Finance

shaping success in business and finance

**(b) Fraud and External/Internal Audit** 6 marks. 1 for internal audit work and 1 for external audit. Maximum 2 per point

Main reason for audit work
Materiality
Identification of fraud
Other relevant points

**Maximum marks**      **6**

**(c) Use of Expert** 6 marks. 1 mark per valid point.

| | |
|---|---|
| Qualification | 1 |
| Experience | 1 |
| References | 1 |
| Project management skills | 1 |
| Access to information | 1 |
| Acceptance by other staff | 1 |
| Other relevant points (each) | 1 |

**Maximum marks**      **6**

**5 (a) Fire at Warehouse**

**(i) Audit Procedures** 5 marks. 1 per well-explained point.

| | |
|---|---|
| Discuss the matter with the directors | 1 |
| Letter of representation point | 1 |
| Schedule of inventory destroyed – reasonable? | 1 |
| Insurance | 1 |
| Going concern status of company | 1 |
| Other relevant points (each) | 1 |

**Maximum marks**      **4**

**(ii) Amendment to Financial Statements** 2 marks. 1 per well-explained point

Disclosure in FS – unlikely with reason
No amendment to B/S etc
Other relevant points

**Maximum marks**      **3**

**(iii) Modification of Audit Report** 3 marks. 1 per well-explained point

| | |
|---|---|
| Modification of report | 1 |
| Going concern status | 1 |
| Inadequate disclosure by directors | 1 |
| Other relevant points (each) | 1 |

**Maximum marks**      **3**

London
School of Business
& Finance

shaping success in business and finance

## (b) Batch of Cheese

### (i) Audit Procedures 5 marks for fire. I per well-explained point.

| | |
|---|---:|
| Discuss with directors | I |
| Copy of damages claim | I |
| Legal advice | I |
| Press reports (or other third party) on cheese | I |
| Going concern? | I |
| Other relevant points (each) | I |

**Maximum marks**     **4**

### (ii) Amendment to Financial Statements 2 marks. I per well-explained point

| | |
|---|---:|
| Disclosure event – because significant impact | I |
| No adjustment | I |
| Going concern issue – reputation | I |
| May result in amendment to FS | I |
| Other relevant points (each) | I |

**Maximum marks**     **3**

### (iii) Modification of Audit Report – 3 marks I per well-explained point

| | |
|---|---:|
| Preparation of FS breakup basis | I |
| Prepared going concern basis – emphasis of matter to note this | I |
| Prepared going concern – but in doubt – emphasis of matter to note this | I |
| Prepared going concern and disagree – qualify report | I |

**Maximum marks**     **3**

# F8

## Examinable Documents

# Examinable Documents June 2009 and December 2009

## AUDIT

## INTERNATIONAL

Knowledge of new examinable regulations issued by 30th September will be examinable in examination sessions being held in the following calendar year. Documents may be examinable even if the effective date is in the future. This means that all regulations issued by 30th September 2008 will be examinable in the June and December 2009 examinations.

The Study Guide offers more detailed guidance on the depth and level at which the examinable documents should be examined. The Study Guide should therefore be read in conjunction with the examinable documents list.

# Accounting Standards

PAPER F8 AUDIT AND ASSURANCE

The accounting knowledge that is assumed for Paper F8 is the same as that examined in Paper F3. Therefore, candidates studying for Paper F8 should refer to the Accounting Standards listed under Paper F3.

PAPER P7 ADVANCED AUDIT AND ASSURANCE

The accounting knowledge that is assumed for Paper P7 is the same as that examined in Paper P2. Therefore, candidates studying for Paper P7 should refer to the Accounting Standards listed under Paper P2.

N.B. P7 will only expect knowledge of accounting standards and financial reporting standards from Paper P2. Knowledge of exposure drafts and discussion papers will not be expected.

| | TITLE | F8 | P7 |
|---|---|---|---|
| | **International Standards on Auditing (ISAs) (UK and Ireland)** | | |
| | Glossary of Terms | 4 | 4 |
| | International Framework for Assurance Assignments | 4 | 4 |
| | Preface to the International Standards on Quality Control, Auditing, Review, Other Assurance and Related Services | 4 | 4 |
| ISA 200 | Objective and General Principles Governing an Audit of Financial Statements | 4 | 4 |
| ISA 210 | Terms of Audit Engagements | 4 | 4 |
| ISA 220 | Quality Control for Audits of Historical Financial Information | | 4 |
| ISA 230 | (Redrafted) Audit Documentation | 4 | 4 |
| ISA 240 | (Redrafted) The Auditor's Responsibilities Relating to Fraud in an Audit of Financial Statements | 4 | 4 |
| ISA 250 | (Redrafted) Consideration of Laws and Regulations in an Audit of Financial Statements | 4 | 4 |
| ISA 260 | (Revised and Redrafted) Communication with Those Charged with Governance | 4 | 4 |
| ISA 300 | (Redrafted) Planning an Audit of Financial Statements | 4 | 4 |
| ISA 315 | (Redrafted) Identifying and Assessing the Risks of Material Misstatement Through Understanding the Entity and Its Environment | 4 | 4 |
| ISA 320 | Audit Materiality | 4 | 4 |
| ISA 330 | (Redrafted) The Auditor's Responses to Assessed Risks | 4 | 4 |

| | TITLE | F8 | P7 |
|---|---|---|---|
| ISA 402 | Audit Considerations Relating to Entities Using Service Organisations | 4 | 4 |
| ISA 500 | Audit Evidence | 4 | 4 |
| ISA 501 | Audit Evidence – Additional Considerations for Specific Items | 4 | 4 |
| ISA 505 | External Confirmations | 4 | 4 |
| ISA 510 | (Redrafted) Audit Engagements – Opening Balances | 4 | 4 |
| ISA 520 | Analytical Procedures | 4 | 4 |
| ISA 530 | Audit Sampling and Other Means of Testing | 4 | 4 |
| ISA 540 | (Revised and Redrafted) Auditing Accounting Estimates, Including Fair Value Estimates and Related Disclosures | 4 | 4 |
| ISA 545 | Auditing Fair Value Measurements and Disclosures | | 4 |
| ISA 550 | (Revised and Redrafted) Related Parties | | 4 |
| ISA 560 | (Redrafted) Subsequent Events | 4 | 4 |
| ISA 570 | (Redrafted) Going Concern | 4 | 4 |
| ISA 580 | (Revised and Redrafted) Written Representations | 4 | 4 |
| ISA 600 | (Revised and Redrafted) Special Considerations - Audits of Group Financial Statement (Including the Work of Component Auditors) | | 4 |
| ISA 610 | Considering the Work of Internal Auditing | 4 | 4 |
| ISA 620 | Using the Work of an Expert | 4 | 4 |
| ISA 700 | The Independent Auditor's Report on a Complete Set of General Purpose Financial Statements | 4 | 4 |
| ISA 701 | Modifications to the Independent Auditor's Report | 4 | 4 |
| ISA 710 | Comparatives | 4 | 4 |
| ISA 720 | (Redrafted) The Auditor's Responsibility in Relation to Other Information in Documents Containing Audited Financial Statements | 4 | 4 |
| ISA 800 | The Auditor's Report on Special Purpose Audit Engagements | | 4 |
| **International Auditing Practice Statements (IAPSs)** | | | |
| IAPS 1000 | Inter-bank Confirmation Procedures | 4 | |
| IAPS 1010 | The Consideration of Environmental Matters in the Audit of Financial Statements | | 4 |
| IAPS 1013 | Electronic Commerce: Effect on the Audit of Financial Statements | 4 | 4 |
| IAPS 1014 | Reporting by Auditors on Compliance with International Financial Reporting Standards | 4 | 4 |
| **International Standards on Assurance Engagements (ISAEs)** | | | |
| ISAE 3000 | Assurance Engagements Other Than Audits or Reviews of Historical Financial Information | 4 | 4 |
| ISAE 3400 | The Examination of Prospective Financial Information | | 4 |
| **International Standards on Quality Control (ISQCs)** | | | |
| ISQC 1 | Quality Control for Firms that Perform Audits and Reviews of Historical Financial Information and Other Assurance and Related Services Engagements | | 4 |
| **International Standards on Related Services (ISRSs)** | | | |
| ISRS 4400 | Engagements to Perform Agreed-Upon Procedures Regarding Financial Information | | 4 |
| ISRS 4410 | Engagements to Compile Financial Information | | 4 |

| | TITLE | F8 | P7 |
|---|---|---|---|
| | **International Standards on Review Engagements (ISREs)** | | |
| ISRE 2400 | Engagements to Review Financial Statements | 4 | 4 |
| ISRE 2410 | Review of Interim Financial Information Performed by the Independent Auditor of the Entity | | 4 |
| | **Exposure Drafts (EDs)** | | |
| | **Other Documents** | | |
| | ACCA's 'Code of Ethics and Conduct' | 4 | 4 |
| | IFAC's 'Code of Ethics for Professional Accountants' | | 4 |
| | ACCA's Technical Factsheet 94 – Anti Money-Laundering (Proceeds of Crime and Terrorism) | | 4 |
| | The Combined Code (of the Committee on Corporate Governance) as an example of a code of best practice | 4 | |
| | Background Information on the Clarity Project of the International Auditing and Assurance Standards Board (IAASB) | | 4 |
| | Status of the IAASB's Work to Clarify the Status of its Standards (IAASB document) | | 4 |

NOTE: Topics of exposure drafts are examinable to the extent that relevant articles about them are published in *Student Accountant*.

# Examinable Documents June 2009 and December 2009

**AUDIT**

**UK**

Knowledge of new examinable regulations issued by 30th September will be examinable in examination sessions being held in the following calendar year. Documents may be examinable even if the effective date is in the future. This means that all regulations issued by 30th September 2008 will be examinable in the June and December 2009 examinations.

The Study Guide offers more detailed guidance on the depth and level at which the examinable documents should be examined. The Study Guide should therefore be read in conjunction with the examinable documents list.

## Accounting Standards

PAPER F8 AUDIT AND ASSURANCE

The accounting knowledge that is assumed for Paper F8 is the same as that examined in Paper F3. Therefore, candidates studying for Paper F8 should refer to the Accounting Standards listed under Paper F3.

PAPER P7 ADVANCED AUDIT AND ASSURANCE

The accounting knowledge that is assumed for Paper P7 is the same as that examined in Paper P2. Therefore, candidates studying for Paper P7 should refer to the Accounting Standards listed under Paper P2.

N.B. P7 will only expect knowledge of accounting standards and financial reporting standards from Paper P2. Knowledge of exposure drafts and discussion papers will not be expected.

| | TITLE | F8 | P7 |
|---|---|---|---|
| | **International Standards on Auditing (ISAs) (UK and Ireland)** | | |
| | Glossary of terms 2008 | 4 | 4 |
| ISA 200 | Objective and General Principles Governing an Audit of Financial Statements | 4 | 4 |
| ISA 210 | Terms of Audit Engagements | 4 | 4 |
| ISA 220 | Quality Control for Audits of Historical Financial Information | | 4 |
| ISA 230 | (Revised) Audit Documentation | 4 | 4 |
| ISA 240 | The Auditor's Responsibility to Conside rFraud in an Audit of Financial Statements | 4 | 4 |
| ISA 250 | Consideration of Laws and Regulations in an Audit of Financial Statements | 4 | 4 |
| ISA 260 | Communication of Audit Matters with Those Charged with Governance | 4 | 4 |
| ISA 300 | Planning an Audit of Financial Statements | 4 | 4 |
| ISA 315 | Obtaining an Understanding of the Entity and its Environment and Assessing the Risks of Material Misstatement | 4 | 4 |
| ISA 320 | Audit Materiality | 4 | 4 |
| ISA 330 | The Auditor's Procedures in Response to Assessed Risks | 4 | 4 |
| ISA 402 | Audit Considerations Relating to Entities Using Service Organisations | 4 | 4 |
| ISA 500 | Audit Evidence | 4 | 4 |
| ISA 501 | Audit Evidence – Additional Considerations for Specific Items | 4 | 4 |
| ISA 510 | Initial Engagements – Opening Balances and Continuing Engagements – | 4 | 4 |

| | TITLE | F8 | P7 |
|---|---|---|---|
| | **Opening Balances** | | |
| ISA 520 | Analytical Procedures | ✔ | ✔ |
| ISA 530 | Audit Sampling and Other Means of Testing | ✔ | ✔ |
| ISA 540 | Audit of Accounting Estimates | ✔ | ✔ |
| ISA 545 | Auditing Fair Value Measurements and Disclosures | | ✔ |
| ISA 550 | Related Parties | | ✔ |
| ISA 560 | Subsequent Events | ✔ | ✔ |
| ISA 570 | Going Concern | ✔ | ✔ |
| ISA 580 | Management Representations | ✔ | ✔ |
| ISA 600 | Using the Work of Another Auditor | | ✔ |
| ISA 610 | Considering the Work of Internal Audit | ✔ | ✔ |
| ISA 620 | Using the Work of an Expert | ✔ | ✔ |
| ISA 700 | The Auditor's Report on Financial Statements | ✔ | ✔ |
| ISA 710 | Comparatives | ✔ | ✔ |
| ISA 720 | (Revised) Section A - Other Information in Documents Containing Audited Financial Statements; Section B – The Auditor's Statutory Reporting Responsibility in Relation to Directors' Reports | ✔ | ✔ |
| | **International Standards on Quality Control (ISQC)** | | |
| ISQC 1 | Quality Control for Firms that Perform Audits and Reviews of Historical Financial Information and Other Assurance and Related Services Engagements | | ✔ |
| | **Practice Notes (PNs)** | | |
| PN 12 | (Revised) Money Laundering – Interim Guidance for Auditors on UK Legislation | | ✔ |
| PN 16 | Bank Reports for Audit Purposes in the United Kingdom (Revised) | ✔ | ✔ |
| PN 22 | The Auditor's Consideration of FRS 17 – 'Retirement Benefits' – Defined Benefit Schemes | | ✔ |
| PN 23 | Auditing Derivative Financial Instruments | | ✔ |
| PN 25 | Attendance at Stocktaking | ✔ | ✔ |
| PN 26 | Guidance for Smaller Entity Documentation | ✔ | ✔ |
| | **Ethical Standards (ESs)** | | |
| ES | (Revised) Provisions Available for Small Entities | ✔ | ✔ |
| ES1 | (Revised) Integrity, Objectivity and Independence | ✔ | ✔ |
| ES2 | (Revised) Financial, Business, Employment and Personal Relationships | ✔ | ✔ |
| ES3 | (Revised) Long Association with the Audit Engagement | ✔ | ✔ |
| ES4 | (Revised) Fees, Remuneration and Evaluation Policies, Litigation, Gifts and Hospitality | ✔ | ✔ |
| ES5 | (Revised) Non-Audit Services Provided to Audit Clients | ✔ | ✔ |
| ESRA | Ethical Standard for Reporting Accountants | ✔ | ✔ |
| | Glossary | ✔ | ✔ |

| | TITLE | F8 | P7 |
|---|---|---|---|
| | **Bulletins** | | |
| 2001/03 | E-business: Identifying Financial Statement Risks | ✔ | ✔ |
| 2006/5 | The Combined Code on Corporate Governance: Requirements of Auditors under the Listing Rules of the Financial Services Authority and the Irish Stock Exchange | ✔ | |
| 2006/6 | Auditor's Reports on Financial Statements in the United Kingdom | ✔ | ✔ |
| 2007/1 | Example Reports by Auditors under Company Legislation in Great Britain | ✔ | ✔ |
| 2008/03 | The Auditor's Statement on the Summary Financial Statement in the United Kingdom | | ✔ |
| 2008/04 | The Special Auditor's Report on Abbreviated Accounts in the United Kingdom | | ✔ |
| 2008/05 | Auditor's Reports on Revised Accounts and Reports in the United Kingdom | ✔ | ✔ |
| 2008/06 | The 'Senior Statutory Auditor' under the United Kingdom Companies Act 2006 | ✔ | ✔ |
| 2008/08 | Auditor's Reports for Short Accounting Periods in Compliance with the United Kingdom Companies Act 2006 | ✔ | ✔ |
| | **Statement of Standards for Reporting Accountants (SSRAs)** | | |
| | Audit Exemption Reports | | ✔ |
| SSRA (UK and Ireland) 2410 | Review of Interim Financial Information Performed by the Independent Auditor of the Entity | | ✔ |
| | **Exposure Drafts (EDs) (UK and Ireland)** | | |
| ISA 700 | (Revised) The Auditor's Report on Financial Statements | | ✔ |
| ISA 720 | (Revised) | | ✔ |
| | Consultation Papers: Guidance for Smaller Entity Audits | | ✔ |
| | Consultation Papers: Auditing Standards Relevant to Group Audits | | ✔ |
| | Discussion Paper: The Auditor's Report: A Time for Change | | ✔ |
| | **Other Documents** | | |
| | ACCA's 'Code of Ethics and Conduct' | ✔ | ✔ |
| | IFAC's 'Code of Ethics for Professional Accountants' | | ✔ |
| | Scope and Authority of APB Pronouncements (Revised) 2008 | ✔ | ✔ |
| | ACCA's Technical Factsheet 94 – Anti-Money Laundering (Proceeds of Crime and Terrorism) | | ✔ |
| | IAASB Clarity Project – Background and Current Status | | ✔ |
| | IAASB Clarity Project – The APB's Approach to IAASB 'Clarified' EDs | | ✔ |
| | Background Information on the Clarity Project of the International Auditing and Assurance Standards Board (IAASB document) | | ✔ |

Note:    Topics of exposure drafts are examinable to the extent that relevant articles about them are published in *Student Accountant*.

# Audit and Other Assurance Engagements

London
School of Business
& Finance

shaping success in business and finance

# Context

This chapter introduces the concept of assurance and how it is important within the business environment. Parties such as shareholders, directors and the other users of financial statements such as creditors and investors need assurance over the financial and nonfinancial information produced by companies. This includes the statutory audit of financial statements and other key assurance services such as reviews of systems and internal controls.

# Exam Hints

This area has been examined before in the F8 exam so you should be comfortable with the concepts in this chapter and be able to explain them in your own words.

In June 2008 students were asked to discuss the concept of 'negative assurance' and to explain how and why this differs 'positive assurance'. Marks were given for good explanations of the terms positive and negative assurance and for the reasons why they differ.

# Key Learning Points

- The statutory audit is a specific type of assurance engagement whereby the external auditors provide reasonable (positive) assurance to the shareholders of a company that the Financial Statements are true and fair.

- The amount of work done by an assurance provider will affect the level of assurance that is given in an assurance report.

- Positive (reasonable) assurance is a high level of assurance but is not a 100% guarantee.

# Chapter Overview

This chapter:
- discusses the concept of assurance;
- explains the difference between the statutory audit and other types of assurance engagement;
- explains the terms positive and negative assurance;
- introduces the statutory audit process.

# I. Assurance

## I.I THE CONCEPT OF ASSURANCE

The concept of assurance is something we come across often in every day life. We ask for assurance when we need to know whether or not things are 'ok'.

Is this house I am about to buy structurally sound or about to fall down?

Is this restaurant safe to eat in?

Is this car safe to drive?

Often it is not possible to check a situation for ourselves so we rely on someone else (usually an expert) to do it for us.

We employ a buildings surveyor to assess our potential new home before we sign the sales contract.

Restaurants have health and safety checks by specialist environmental health officers.

It is a legal requirement in the UK for cars to pass an MOT carried out by a qualified mechanic.

These are all examples of **assurance**.

## I.2 ASSURANCE IN THE BUSINESS ENVIRONMENT

Assurance is a concept that is also widely used in the business environment. For example:

- Shareholders need assurance that the published financial statements of a company are accurate, so external auditors check these financial statements (this is known as the statutory audit and is covered in detail later).
- Directors need assurance that the systems inside a company are working so internal auditors check these systems.

These are all examples of **assurance engagements**.

**Definition**

> **Assurance Engagement** - An assurance engagement is one in which an assurance provider (practitioner) expresses a conclusion designed to enhance the degree of confidence of the intended users, other than the responsible party, about the outcome of the evaluation or measurement of a subject matter against suitable criteria.

## I.3 THE FEATURES OF AN ASSURANCE ENGAGEMENT

Although each assurance engagement will differ in terms of the exact detail, each has common features.

- There is a **subject matter** – what is it we are checking?
- There are **three main parties** involved:
  - the **responsible person** – the person who prepares the subject matter being checked;
  - the **assurance provider (practitioner)** – the party who forms the opinion on the subject matter and gives the assurance;
  - the **intended user** – the party who relies on the assurance report.
- A **report** will be written stating the assurance provider's conclusion. The intended users can read this report to get their assurance.
- The assurance provider doing the checks will have some standards to check against.
- The amount of checking (work) will have to be decided.

## I.4 LEVELS OF ASSURANCE: POSITIVE AND NEGATIVE ASSURANCE

As noted above, the amount of work done by the practitioner can vary and this will affect the **level of assurance** that is provided. Depending upon the amount and the nature of the work performed, the assurance provider will give either **positive (reasonable)** or **negative** assurance.

### 1.4.1 POSITIVE (REASONABLE) ASSURANCE

If a lot of detailed work is performed on the subject matter, the assurance provider can conclude whether or not the subject matter has been properly prepared.

Positive assurance is a **high** level of assurance so a high level of reliance can be placed upon it. Positive assurance however is not a 100% guarantee.

Imagine taking your car to a garage. If the mechanic does a lot of detailed testing on the main parts of the car (engine, breaks, exhaust, radiator etc) he or she will be able to give you a high level of assurance that your car is working properly. And in turn you could place a high level of reliance on this. We would call this positive assurance. What the mechanic will not do is take apart every nut and bolt and give you a 100% guarantee that your car is free from problems – this would be impractical.

An example of positive assurance is given in the statutory audit report. In their conclusion auditors say **'in our opinion the financial statements give (or do not give) a true and fair view of the state of the company's affairs'.**

### 1.4.2 NEGATIVE ASSURANCE

If a smaller amount of work is performed on the subject matter then the assurance provider may only be able to confirm that 'nothing has come to light to suggest errors or problems exist'. In other words, there may be inaccuracies/problems, however, the assurance providers did not come across them! This is a much lower level of assurance and is known as **negative assurance**. Obviously less reliance should be placed on negative assurance.

## Different Types of Assurance Engagement

The syllabus distinguishes between two main types of assurance engagement:

* the external (statutory) audit;
* internal audit and other types of assurance services.

### 1.5 THE EXTERNAL (STATUTORY) AUDIT

Company directors are responsible for producing Financial Statements and the shareholders need to be assured that they are accurate.

In most countries it is a **statutory (legal) requirement** for a team of auditors (qualified accountants) from outside the company to come in to check the financial statements on behalf of the shareholders. The auditors give the shareholders assurance that the financial statements are:

* true and Fair and;
* properly prepared in accordance with the relevant accounting standards and legal framework.

This is known as the **statutory audit.**

## Definition:

**IFAC Definition of an Audit** - The objective of an audit of the financial statements is to enable the auditor to express and opinion on whether or not the financial statements are prepared, in all material respects, in accordance with an applicable financial reporting framework. The phrases used to express the auditor's opinion are 'give a true and fair view' or 'present fairly in all material respects', which are equivalent terms.

## Definitions:

**True** - The financial statements are factual and are free from material error.

**Fair** - The financial statements are free from bias and reflect the commercial substance of the transactions that have taken place.

**Materiality** - An item is material if it is important enough to affect the users of the financial statements. This could be due to its size or its very nature (there is much more on materiality in later chapters).

In the UK most companies over a certain size are required to have their financial statements audited in accordance with the Companies Act 2006.

The criteria that the auditors will use to check the Financial Statements are the Accounting Standards (and in the UK the Companies Act 2006).

The final outcome of a statutory audit is an **audit report**, which is addressed to the **shareholders** and contains the auditor's **opinion** as to whether or not the financial statements give a true and fair view.

## Background: The need for statutory audit and agency theory

Some companies (often smaller companies) are run on a day-to-day basis by their owners (shareholders). For the vast majority of companies however (especially larger companies), a team of directors will be appointed to run the company on the shareholders' behalf. These directors act as stewards of the company and as a result they are accountable to the shareholders.

The directors are responsible for producing periodical financial statements (typically at the end of each twelve month period). These financial statements set out the position and performance of the company. As most shareholders are not involved in the day-to-day running of their company or the production of these statements how do they know that these financial statements are accurate and unbiased? How do they know whether or not to trust the directors?

This is where the statutory audit comes in. The **financial statements** are subject to checks by an independent and knowledgeable third party **(i.e. the auditors)** to give the shareholders the assurance they need.

You may often hear both the directors and the auditors referred to as **agents**. An agent is a person used to provide a particular service.

The directors act as agents for the shareholders by running the company on their behalf. The auditors act as agents for the shareholders, by giving them assurance over the financial statements.

### 1.5.1 THE STATUTORY AUDIT: LEVEL OF ASSURANCE

The level of assurance provided by a statutory audit report is always **positive (reasonable)**. In order to provide such a level of assurance the auditors must carry out extensive and detailed checks on the financial statements, which will include:

- assessing risk;
- planning procedures;
- conducting procedures;
- assessing results;
- expressing an opinion.

Because Financial Statements are based upon historic information, the auditor should be able to obtain the evidence they need to give assurance that they are correct; hence the use of positive assurance.

The statutory audit will never give a 100% guarantee that the financial statements are true and fair. This results from factors such as:

- The **inherent limitations** in audit including:
  - the use of testing;
  - the inherent limitations of internal control;
  - the fact that most audit evidence is persuasive rather than conclusive;
  - the impracticality of testing all transactions;
  - the possibility of fraud.

London School of Business & Finance
shaping success in business and finance

- The fact that audit work is permeated by **judgement** e.g.
  - judging the amount of audit evidence required to give the opinion;
  - concluding on estimates and **judgements** made by the directors.

### 1.5.2   *INTERNATIONAL STANDARDS ON AUDITING (ISA'S)*

The International Standards on Auditing (ISAs) contain the **guidance and rules** that auditors must follow when auditing historical financial information. The ISA's are set by the International Audit and Assurance Standards Board (IAASB), which is part of the International Federation of Accountants (IFAC).

# Learning Example 1

The statutory audit is a specific type of assurance engagement. Using it as an example, fill in the following blanks. The first has been done to help you.

**Subject matter**                                   *Financial Statements*

**Responsible party**

**Assurance provider**

**Intended user**

**Level of assurance provided**

## 1.6   INTERNAL AUDIT AND OTHER ASSURANCE SERVICES

We have now been introduced to the specific assurance engagement that is the statutory audit however there are plenty of other areas over which stakeholders in a company may seek assurance even though it is not required by law.

For example:

- Directors are looking to raise finance from the company's bankers and have produced a cash-flow forecast that the bank will rely on when making their decision. They wish to be assured that this forecast is reasonable.
- A company has many complex internal systems and controls to help prevent fraud and errors and wish to be assured that these systems are working.

In these cases sufficient assurance may be obtained from a less detailed engagement for example a **review**. As with a statutory audit, a report will be issued to the users containing the assurance provider's conclusions. It is very important to note that a review would involve less detailed testing than a statutory audit and this in turn will affect the **level of assurance** that the user could gain.

### 1.6.1   *INTERNAL AUDIT*

In order to perform these other types of assurance engagements, many company directors will appoint their own internal function. This function is usually staffed by a team of auditors from within the company itself however, in some cases, this function can be outsourced to an external party.

### Definition

**Internal Audit** - Internal auditing is an appraisal, or monitoring activity, established within an entity as a service to the entity.

The functions of internal audit can include one or more of the following:

- monitoring of internal control;
- examination of financial and operating information;
- review of the economy, efficiency and effectiveness of a company's operations;
- review of compliance with laws and regulations;
- special investigations e.g. suspected fraud.

*Important note: This exam paper is aimed at understanding the work done by both external and internal auditors, with the majority of the syllabus aimed at the work of <u>external auditors</u>.*

1.7   COMPARISON OF INTERNAL AND EXTERNAL AUDITING

|  | **External Audit** | **Internal Audit** |
|---|---|---|
| Appointed by | Shareholders for statutory audit | Directors |
| Reporting to | Shareholders for statutory audit | Directors |
| What they check | Annual Financial Statements for statutory audit | Determined by directors but mainly internal systems and controls |
| Legal requirement | Yes for statutory audit | Typically no |
| Independence | Must be independent | Ideally should be independent but hard to achieve |

1.8   THE IMPORTANCE OF INDEPENDENCE IN ASSURANCE

Assurance reports are written for the benefit of the people reading them. The readers need to be able to trust that the reports are reliable and correct. If they sense any links between the auditors and the things being audited, they may not trust the opinions given.

If there are any links between the auditors and the things being audited the report loses credibility and the assurance is undermined.

It is therefore a requirement that that auditors are **independent** of those they are auditing.

# Learning Example 2

You are the external auditors of Zafiro Limited which designs and manufactures parts for car engines and supplies to many of the major car manufacturers in the UK. Zafiro has invested heavily in research and development in recent years and has recently developed a new engine part that can help cars use fuel more efficiently. Many of its suppliers have expressed an interest in purchasing this new engine part but in order to meet demand, Zafiro will need to expand its production line and employ five new members of staff.

Zafiro has approached its bank about obtaining a loan to help fund the expansion and the bank have asked to see a profit and loss forecast for the next five years before they will make a decision as to whether or not to provide the loan. Zafiro's directors have completed the forecast but have asked you as external auditors to review and report on the forecast before it is presented to the bank.

Explain what **level of assurance** this report on the cash-flow forecast will give to the directors and explain **how and why** this level of assurance differs to that given in a statutory audit report.

1.9   THE EXTERNAL AUDIT PROCESS – AN OVERVIEW

We have covered the fundamental concepts of audit and assurance so now we begin to look at the external (statutory) audit process in more detail.

All external audits follow a similar process from start to finish, from appointment of the auditors to the issuing of the final audit report. This process is introduced briefly below. In later chapters, each step is discussed in more detail.

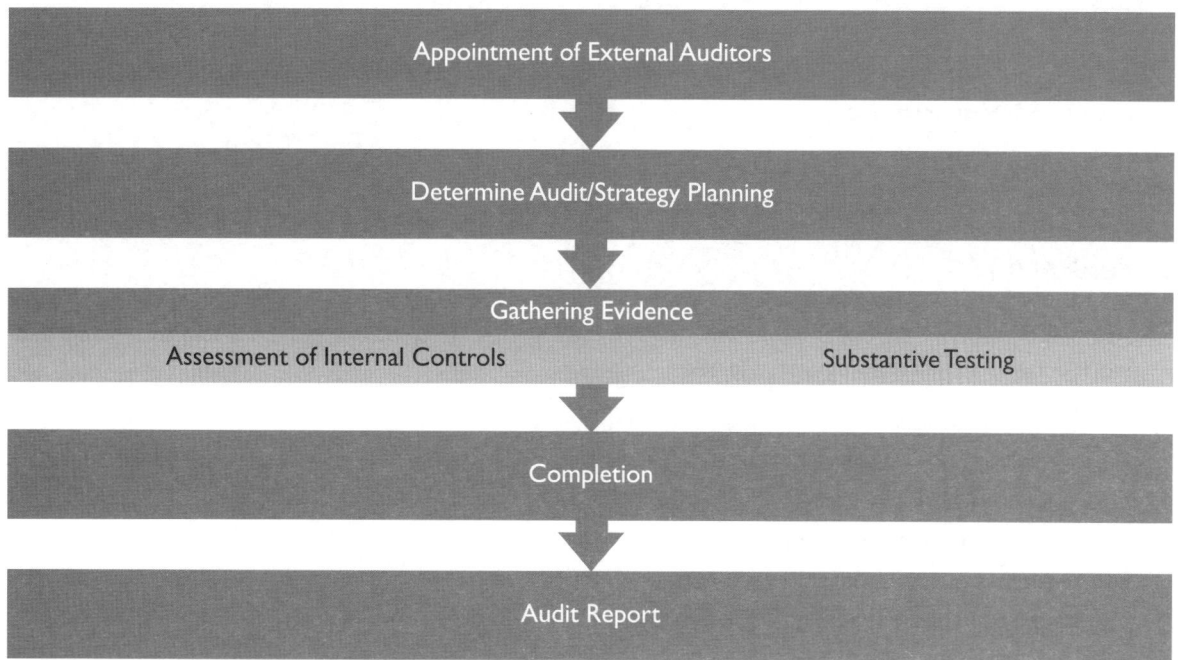

### 1.9.1 APPOINTMENT OF EXTERNAL AUDITORS

Tendering is the most common way of auditors winning business. Although auditors may be invited to tender by the directors it its ultimately the **shareholders** who approve the appointment.

Before accepting appointment the auditors must consider their **independence** and this is discussed in detail in chapter 2.

### 1.9.2 DETERMINE AUDIT STRATEGY/PLANNING

Having accepted appointment the auditors must plan their work. Amongst other things, this involves an assessment of **risk**.

### 1.9.3 ASSESSMENT OF INTERNAL CONTROLS

Companies have many internal systems and it is from these systems that the numbers in the financial statements are derived, for example sales system, payroll system, purchases system. In each of these systems, a number of **internal controls** will operate. The internal controls are the measures put in place by the directors of the company to help prevent and detect errors within the systems.

It is very important that auditors assess the strength of these internal controls, as this will affect the amount of detailed testing that they will have to do on the financial statements later.

**Let's take the sales system as an example.**

If the controls operating over the sales system are strong, the auditors can be reasonably sure that the numbers produced by that system (i.e. sales and trade receivables) are correct. This will mean less detailed testing needs to be performed on these numbers later.

On the other hand, if the controls over the sales system are weak, then auditors will be far less confident that the numbers coming out of the sales system are correct. This means that more detailed testing will need to be carried out on these numbers later. These detailed tests are known as substantive tests.

### 1.9.4 *SUBSTANTIVE TESTING*

As mentioned above, the amount of substantive testing to be done is determined by the assessment of the company's internal controls.

- **Strong** controls leads to **reduced** substantive testing.
- **Weak** controls leads to **increased** substantive testing.

### 1.9.5 *COMPLETION*

At the completion stage the auditors bring everything together. They consider the financial statements and the work done to support the opinion and ask:

- Was the work done in line with the audit plan?
- Has the right work been done?
- Has enough work been done?
- Are there any unresolved issues?
- Do the financial statements make sense?
- Has the audit report been drafted correctly?

### 1.9.6 *AUDIT REPORT*

The final stage in the process is for the auditors to give their opinion on the financial statements. This is contained in the **audit report**, which is addressed to the shareholders.

### 1.10 THE EXTERNAL AUDIT TIMELINE – INTERIM AND FINAL AUDITS

Once the external auditors have been appointed, when does all of the audit work take place? Six months, three months, one month before the financial year end? One month, two months after the year end?

Generally the answer to this depends upon the size and nature of the company being audited. It is important to note however that despite that, there are **key events** for the auditors during each year, which you need to be aware of.

### 1.10.1 *INTERIM AUDIT*

The interim audit will take place before the financial year- end.

The financial statements are not yet available at this point so the interim audit will focus on the detailed audit planning and assessment of internal which can be done without waiting for the accounting year to end.

On very large audits, more than one interim visit may be necessary.

### 1.10.2 *FINANCIAL YEAR END*

When the financial year comes to an end and the directors will begin the process of producing that year's financial statements,

It is too early for auditors to carry out lots of testing at this point however, a number of audit procedures can take place:

- attend client's year end stock take;
- perform a debtor's circularisation;
- request a bank letter.

### 1.10.3 *FINAL AUDIT*

The draft (unaudited) Financial Statements will now be available. The main focus is substantive testing – results of controls testing determine how much substantive testing is required.

1.10.4 *REPORTING DEADLINE*

Sometime after the final audit has commenced, the auditors will conclude their work and issue their audit report to the shareholders.

**The Audit Timeline - Illustration**

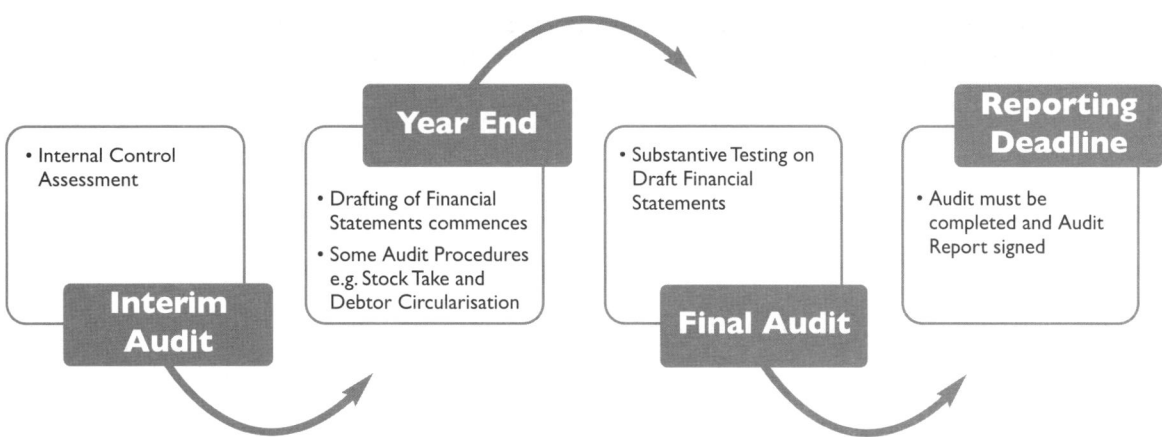

## Solution to Learning Example 1

| | |
|---|---|
| **Subject matter** | *Financial Statements* |
| **Responsible party** | *Directors* |
| **Assurance provider** | *External auditors* |
| **Intended user** | *Shareholders* |
| **Level of assurance provided** | *Positive/Reasonable* |

## Solution to Learning Example 2

### Level of assurance

The forecast is based on assumptions of future income and expenses. Any predictions of this nature are uncertain and involve a significant amount of judgement. It would not be possible for the auditors to give a positive confirmation that the information is free from error so the level of assurance provided by this report would be **negative**.

### How it differs to statutory audit

The level of assurance given by a statutory audit report is **positive** (or reasonable) assurance. This is a high level of assurance.

### Why it differs

The statutory audit is based on the **historic** information in the financial statements. The auditors will be able to collect sufficient evidence to prove whether or not this information is correct and thereby give a high level of assurance. The review on the other hand, is based upon assumptions of the **future** for which evidence is not yet available. The level of assurance provided in this case must naturally be lower.

In addition, during a statutory audit a lot of detailed testing is done on the financial statements whereas for the review the level of testing is likely to be much lower. This difference in the amount of work performed will affect the level of assurance given in each case.

## Learning Summary

- Make sure you can explain the terms 'statutory audit', 'positive assurance' and 'negative assurance' in your own words without reference to your notes.

- Complete the learning examples in Chapter 1.

- Go to **http://annualreport.marksandspencer.com/financials/auditors_report.html** and read through the statutory audit report for Marks & Spencer. Highlight and explain any familiar terms you have come across in this chapter such as 'independent', 'reasonable assurance' 'true and fair' etc.

# 2

# Audit Ethics and Regulation

# Context

Before auditors accept appointment to a client there are a number of very important considerations. Firstly, they need to fulfil certain legal requirements with regards to their qualifications and the appointment process. Secondly, it is vital that they are independent from the client so they need to comply with relevant ethical guidelines. This chapter takes you through the legal requirements that auditors need to fulfil, discusses the issues that may threaten auditor's independence and outlines the safeguards that audit firms can put in place to ensure they remain independent from their clients. We will then go on to consider acceptance and the engagement letter.

# Exam Hints

Audit ethics and regulation is a vital part of the syllabus and will be highly likely to feature in the exam.

In December 2007 students were asked to explain the ACCA's five fundamental ethical principles as part of a knowledge question. In December 2008, students were presented with a scenario and asked to identify threats to the auditor's independence and recommend appropriate safeguards.

# Key Learning Points

- The ACCA's Code of Ethics and Conduct set out five fundamental principles for auditors, which are objectivity, professional behaviour, technical competence, integrity and confidentiality.
- Auditors may encounter threats to their ability to remain independent and these threats tend to fall into one of six categories; self interest, self-review, advocacy, familiarity, intimidation and management threats.
- Auditors must keep client information confidential unless they have a right or duty to disclose it to third parties.
- Once auditors have been appointed it is vital that they issue an engagement letter. The engagement letter is the contract between the auditors and the client and it reduces the risk of misunderstandings.

# Chapter Overview

This chapter covers:

- ethics;
- the legal aspects of appointment;
- engagement letters.

APPOINTMENT OF EXTERNAL AUDITORS

Before auditors accept appointment to a client there are a number of very important considerations:

- ethical considerations;
- legal considerations;
- the engagement letter.

This chapter shall deal with each in turn.

## 2. Audit Ethics and Regulation

2.1 ETHICS

Ethics is concerned with **behaviour** and trying to ensure that auditors act in a **professional** manner and stay **independent** from their clients. It is crucial that auditors both:

- **follow** the ethical guidelines; *and*
- are **perceived to be following** the ethical guidelines.

There is a subtle difference, which becomes evident when we consider one of the most notorious accounting scandals of recent times.

Everyone involved in the audit profession will remember the case of the US company Enron and its auditors, Arthur Anderson. In 2001 directors of Enron were discovered to be perpetrating a fraud so huge that that it bankrupted the company and lost millions of dollars of investors' money.

Shortly after the discovery of the fraud, Arthur Anderson was found guilty in the US of obstruction of justice for shredding documents related to the Enron audit and was forced to stop auditing public companies.

In 2005 the conviction was overturned by the US Supreme Court but by this point the reputation of Anderson was already damaged beyond repair due to the perception that they were in the wrong. They were unable to remain a viable business.

2.1.1 *RULES v PRINCIPLES*

Ethics is a difficult area in which to try and impose **prescriptive rules**. Imagine we impose a rule that says auditors cannot accept free lunches from clients as this may pose a threat to independence. Does this mean that they can accept if they are offered free flights to Barbados? The ethical dilemmas auditors face will all differ in their exact detail so it would be unrealistic to create a set of rules that covers every eventuality.

We solve this problem by having ethical **guidance** rather than prescriptive rules. In this case, the guidance may say that we can only accept modest gifts from clients and must refuse all others. The guidance covers a multitude of potential scenarios but it also relies on the auditors to act professionally and apply the guidance appropriately when faced with difficult situations.

2.1.2 *FUNDAMENTAL ETHICAL PRINCIPLES*

An International Code of Ethics has been developed by the International Federation of Accountants (IFAC) with the aim of promoting consistency and providing countries with a starting point for developing their own codes.

In the UK, the Auditing Practices Board (APB) has created a series of Ethical Standards that are based upon the IFAC Code but tailored to the UK market. All UK Institutes, including the ACCA, have adopted these standards.

The ACCA's Code of Ethics and Conduct sets out five fundamental principles with which its members must comply. These are explained on the next page.

| Professional Behaviour | All members of the ACCA should respect the laws and regulations of the profession. They should never act in a manner that would discredit their profession. |
|---|---|
| Integrity | This principle requires members to act in a straightforward and honest manner in all their business and professional relationships. |
| Competence | Members have a duty to maintain their professional knowledge and skills. They should act in accordance with applicable technical and professional standards when providing professional services. |
| Confidentiality | Members should respect the confidentiality of their clients and not disclose any client information to third parties unless they have a legal or professional **right** or **duty** to disclose. There is more on confidentiality later in the chapter. |
| Objectivity | The users of assurance reports need to be confident that the assurance provider's opinion can be relied upon. If the assurance provider is linked to the client in some way there is a risk that the opinion may be biased. It is therefore essential that assurance providers are **independent** of their clients so that they can provide an objective, unbiased opinion. |

### 2.1.3   ETHICAL THREATS

Throughout the course of their work, assurance providers may encounter a wide range of circumstances affecting their ability to comply with the ACCA's Code of Ethics. We call these ethical threats and they generally fall into six distinct categories:

- self-Interest threat;
- self-review threat;
- familiarity threats;
- advocacy threats;
- intimidation threats;
- management threats.

Before accepting clients, auditors must assess any ethical threats and either put in place measures to **mitigate** the threats **(safeguards)** or **reject the appointment**.

We should note however that identification of ethical threats is not just something takes place before accepting a client. Auditors must be continually aware that new threats that may arise during the course of their work and if appropriate safeguards cannot be put in place to mitigate these threats, they may need to consider **resigning** from the engagement.

The different types of threats and the appropriate safeguards are discussed in more detail below.

### 2.1.4   SELF-INTEREST THREATS

Self-interest threats arise when the auditors put their own interests above those of the client or shareholders.

Imagine you own a number of shares in your listed audit client. Shortly after the financial year end you are doing the audit work and you discover a material error in the Financial Statements. You ask the directors to correct the error but they refuse. You know that, as a result, you should qualify the audit opinion in respect of these Financial Statements but you are concerned that this will affect stock-market confidence in your client and subsequently the value of the shares that you own may fall.

Do you qualify the audit opinion? If you don't, you have put your own personal interests above those of the shareholders who need to know that the Financial Statements are materially misstated.

Self-interest threats can also arise when:

- **Auditors receive excessive gifts or hospitality from a client**
  The risk here is that auditors ignore errors in the Financial Statements so as not to upset the client as this may lead to the gifts/hospitality being withdrawn.

- **Auditors receive a large proportion of their fees from one client**
  Auditors may ignore errors in the Financial Statements for fear of losing the client and the associated income.

- **Auditors have personal or business relationships with a client**
  If the auditor has a personal or business relationship with then they may ignore problems with the client's financial statements in order to protect this relationship.

- **Audit fees are agreed on a contingent basis**
  Contingent fees are fees that are dependent on the outcome of the work performed. If audit fees are calculated on this basis, the auditors may be tempted to give an opinion that the directors want, rather than the correct opinion, so as to receive these fees.

- **Auditors and clients lend each other money**
  This relationship is almost certain to threaten an auditor's independence and objectivity. If the client owes the auditor money, the auditor may not want to risk upsetting them with a qualified opinion in case this leads to the client defaulting on the debt.
  Note that in a situation where there are overdue fees, the auditor runs the risk, in effect, of making a loan to a client.

- **Auditors set their fees at an unrealistically low level in order to secure work (also known as low-balling)**
  By setting audit fees at an unrealistically low level in order to win other more lucrative work such as tax advice, auditors risk not being able to resource the audit properly. This could be perceived as negligence.

### 2.1.5 *SAFEGUARDS AGAINST SELF-INTEREST THREATS*

### Financial Interests (e.g. owning shares in a client)

The ACCA does not allow any of following parties to own a direct financial interest in a client or a material indirect financial interest in a client (e.g. by investing in a pension scheme that invests in the client's shares):

- the audit firm;
- a member of the audit team;
- the immediate family of a member of the audit team.

The following safeguards should be put in place:

- dispose of any interest as soon as it is identified;
- remove the individual from the audit team if necessary;
- inform the client of the situation;
- use an independent partner to review any work already carried out.

### Gifts and Hospitality

Gifts and hospitality should not be accepted unless the value is clearly insignificant.

### High Proportion of Fees from One Client

Audit firms should avoid having any one client that makes up a significant proportion of their fee income

| Listed Clients | Gross recurring fees from a single listed client should not be more than 10% of audit firm's total income. When these fees reach 5%, the situation should be reviewed. |
|---|---|
| Non Listed Clients | Gross recurring fees a single non-listed client should not be more than 15% of audit firm's total income. When these fees reach 10% the situation should be reviewed. |

### Close Business or Personal Relationships

An auditor should not participate in a personal or business relationship with a client. If an individual team member has such an interest they should be removed from the audit team.

An **audit partner** should not accept a key management position at an audit client until at least two years have elapsed since his/her involvement in the audit.

### Contingent Fees

Audit firms are not allowed to enter into any fee arrangement that is contingent in nature.

### Loans and Overdue Fees

Audit firms or team members should not enter into any loan relationship with a client.

The only exception to this is where a loan is made to a member of an assurance team by a bank or other lending institution. Providing this loan is on normal commercial terms, this is not perceived to be a threat to independence.

Audit firms should guard against overdue fees and consider resigning when fees remain unpaid.

### Lowballing

If an audit engagement is accepted at a lower than average fee the audit firm must:

- demonstrate that appropriate staff and time are spent on the work;
- comply with the applicable professional and technical standards.

### 2.1.6   SELF-REVIEW THREATS

This threat arises when auditors perform work/produce information for the client that they end up reviewing themselves as part of an assurance engagement.

Imagine you are asked by a client to help with the preparation of the corporation tax figure in financial statements. You are happy to help and then the next week you are back at the client auditing the Financial Statements that contain the tax figure you have calculated. How likely are you to find errors in your own calculation? Are you likely to be objective?

Self-review threats arise when auditors:

- give advice on accounting or control systems and then audit them (e.g. by performing internal audit services for the client);
- prepare financial information or assist with calculations then audit this information;
- provide services for the client e.g. tax, valuation, corporate finance, and then review this work as part of the audit;
- join the audit team after working for the client.

### 2.1.7   SAFEGUARDS AGAINST SELF-REVIEW THREATS

### Provision of Services Other than Audit

Providing a client with services other than audit is a highly controversial issue. In most cases it is fine to provide other services providing **independence and objectivity** are not affected.

Safeguards should be put in place such as:

- the team that performs the audit should be composed of entirely different members to the one that performs the other service;
- an independent second partner review on all work performed;
- refuse the other service if audit objectivity is threatened.

There are however some notable exceptions in terms of the provision of other services:

- auditors should not prepare the accounts or Financial Statements for a listed or public interest client;
- audit firms should not carry out valuations on matters which may be material to the Financial Statements;
- audit firms should not be involved in the design or implementation of an IT system for the client where that IT system is an integral part of the accounting function.

**Client Employee Joins Audit Team**

If, in the previous two years, an individual has been a director of the client or involved in any way with the information being audited they should not be assigned to the audit team.

### 2.1.8   FAMILIARITY THREATS

Familiarity threats arise when the auditors develop a close relationship with the client and as a result become too sympathetic to their interests or too trusting of their work.

> You met Bob, the finance director of your client, almost 10 years ago when you first accepted appointment as auditor. You and Bob have become good friends over this time. So much so, you often play golf together at weekends and you regularly meet up for dinner along with your respective partners.

> Every year as part of your audit procedures you should assess the internal controls in Bob's business. You have been auditing Bob's company for 10 years so perhaps you can rely on your previous assessment and reduce the amount of work you do this year? They were ok in previous years so nothing is likely to have changed has it? And if you do find a problem, do you really want to tell your friend who was responsible for designing and implementing them?

Examples of familiarity threats are:

- the auditor audits a company where friends or relatives work;
- the auditor has been auditing the company many years;
- there are people working at the client who recently worked for the audit form.

### 2.1.9   SAFEGUARDS AGAINST FAMILIARITY THREATS

The ACCA sets out some specific safeguards to help to mitigate familiarity threats:

- no member of the audit team should have a close personal or business relationship with the client.
- also for **listed clients:**
  o the engagement partner should act for no longer than five consecutive years. They should not return to this role until a further five years have elapsed;
  o other key audit partners should act for no longer than seven consecutive years. They should not return to the role until a further two years have elapsed;
  o the person responsible for quality control review on the audit engagement should act for no longer than seven years. They should not return to the role until a further two years have elapsed.
- an **audit partner** should not accept a key management position at an audit client until at least two years have elapsed since his/her involvement in the audit.

### 2.1.10   ADVOCACY THREAT

The advocacy threat arises when auditors fail to take a balanced view on their clients affairs and are perceived to be either 'taking their clients side' or are biased against their client.

> You have been auditing a client for two years and over this time have noticed that their Health and Safely procedures are not entirely adequate. During this year's audit one of your team members in injured while observing the stock-take and you take the client to court to seek damages, as you believe that they are to blame. Will you find it easy to remain objective when you come to giving an opinion on the Financial Statements?

Examples of advocacy threats include:

- representing an audit client in a legal case or tax enquiry;
- taking legal action against a client or being sued by a client.

### 2.1.11  SAFEGUARDS AGAINST ADVOCACY THREATS

Auditors should withdraw from the engagement if they are involved in serious litigation with their client. (Although it is highly likely that the client has removed them as auditors by this point anyway!)

### 2.1.12  INTIMIDATION THREATS

This threat is caused by a client being in a position to put pressure on an auditor to prevent them acting objectively. This could arise from family and personal relationships, litigation or close business relationships. As a result, the intimidation threat is very closely related to the self-interest and the advocacy threat so the safeguards are the same.

### 2.1.13  MANAGEMENT THREAT

As we have heard repeatedly, auditors should be independent of their clients. They should under no circumstances agree to provide services that result in them either:

- acting as management of the client; or
- making management decisions for the client.

If they take on management functions, their independence is threatened.

### 2.1.14  SAFEGUARDS AGAINST THE MANAGEMENT THREAT

Auditors should ensure that the client accepts responsibility for all management decisions, even where the audit firm provides a lot of advice.

When taking on additional work for clients, auditors should ensure that they act in an advisory capacity only and do not make decisions and perform work that is the responsibility of the company's management.

## Learning Example 1

You are one of the partners at the audit firm Miles & Co Chartered Accountants and number of situations have arisen amongst your clients. Miles & Co is a small firm with two partners operating from an office based in London.

**For each scenario below explain the ethical threats in each case and state which safeguards are necessary if your firm is to continue with its appointment.**

- Your brother has just been appointed finance director at your client Jermain Ltd.

- The finance director of Pebbles Beach Wear Ltd has broken his leg playing football and will be unable to work for six weeks. The financial year end is next week and the managing director has asked if the audit team manager will help to prepare the corporation tax calculations.

- In recent years, Bingo UK Ltd has relied on your help to draft their Financial Statements. Appropriate safeguards have always been put in place to mitigate the self-review threat such as separate teams preparing and auditing and independent review of the files by the second partner in the office. In the last few years, Bingo has grown in popularity and as a result Bingo UK has expanded rapidly. They are aiming to list within the next six months.

## 2.2    CONFIDENTIALITY

Generally auditors should never share client information with third parties. There are, however, a small number of situations where auditors may have a **legal duty** or a **right** to disclose client information.

### 2.2.1    *LEGAL DUTY TO DISCLOSE*

Information **must** be disclosed if:

- client is suspected of money laundering;
- client is suspected of terrorism;
- client is suspected of treason;
- the ACCA are investigating the auditors work;
- a court order is obtained requiring the auditors to disclose.

### 2.2.2    *RIGHT TO DISCLOSE*

The auditor **may** decide to disclose information if:

- client gives permission;
- the auditor feels that it is in the public interest to do so.

## 2.3    CONFLICTS OF INTEREST

Auditors must be seen to act in the best interest of their clients at all times. Problems often arise when auditors act for two companies who are in direct competition with each other and particularly when the auditors have access to confidential information about these clients.

**Imagine the following scenario:**

Bekay is a company specialising in pest control, removing rats, mice and squirrels from homes and businesses in the city of Blensville. They are the largest pest control company in the area. Bekay have asked your firm to become their auditors.

There are three other major pest control companies in the area, one of them being Hyper Control who you have audited for many years.

Hyper Control supplied some materials to Bekay last year but Bekay are refusing to pay them as they are questioning the value of the materials supplied. A court case to settle the dispute is due to start next week. If Bekay loses the case they will be ordered to pay the legal costs.

**What problems arise if your firm takes on Bekay as an audit client?**

- As the two companies are direct competitors, any business advice the auditors offer to one client is unlikely to be in the best interests of the other client.

- Confidential information about one of the companies could reach the other. If audit paperwork is not kept secure, or audit staff are not discrete, sensitive information relevant to the dispute could be passed across.

- The auditors may learn for example that Hyper Control is thinking of dropping the case. If so, Bekay will no longer need a provision for the legal costs. How can they tell Bekay to remove the provision without breaching client confidentiality?

### 2.3.1    *DEALING WITH CONFLICTS OF INTEREST*

Before accepting any new appointment auditors must be aware of any potential conflicts of interest.
- If a situation arises where auditors may be acting for direct competitors, **all clients involved should be informed** and give **consent** for the auditors to continue to act.

- If consent is received, auditors should put measures in place to ensure that client information is kept confidential. This may involve measures such as:

  o each client is serviced by different audit teams headed by different partners;

  o the teams are kept physically separated;

  o strict procedures for monitoring confidentiality are put in place – including appointment of an independent partner to oversee the process;

  o strict security over the files of each client;

  o independent review of all audit files before the audit reports are signed.

  You may often see these measures referred to as 'Chinese Walls'.

- If no suitable measures can be put in place or if clients refuse to consent, **declining the appointment (or resigning from an existing one)** may be the only sensible way forward.

## 2.4    LEGAL CONSIDERATIONS

In addition to the ethical issues that auditors must consider, there are also a number of statutory (legal) requirements that must be fulfilled before an external auditor accepts appointment. We shall consider these in turn:

- who is allowed to be an external auditor;
- appointment of external auditors;
- removal of external auditors.

### 2.4.1    *WHO IS ALLOWED TO BE AN EXTERNAL AUDITOR?*

To be allowed to perform external audits, an individual must go through an approval process. The individual must:

- pass an approved set of examinations set by a **Recognised Qualifying Body (RQB)**. Examples of an RQB include the ACCA and the ICAEW;
- become a member (and stay a member) of a **Recognised Supervisory Body (RSB)**. The ACCA and the ICAEW are also examples of RSBs.

In addition, the individual must not be either of:

- **a director or employee** of the client or any of its associated companies;
- **a business partner or employee** of a director or employee of the client, or any of its associated companies.

### 2.4.2    *APPOINTMENT OF EXTERNAL AUDITORS – THE LEGAL PROCESS*

In the vast majority of cases the company's **shareholders** appoint the external auditors.

In practice the Board of Directors will propose an audit firm, which is subject to approval by the shareholders (usually on an annual basis at the company AGM).

Shareholders approve the appointment by passing what is known as an **ordinary resolution**.

An ordinary resolution is a specific legal term.  In order for an ordinary resolution to be passed there are two requirements to be met:

- More than 50% of the shareholder votes must approve the appointment;
- The shareholders must be given 21 days notice that the vote will take place.

In rare cases the auditors are approved by the Board of Directors or, in the UK, the Secretary of State for Business, Enterprise and Regulatory Reform.  .

| **The Board of Directors** | May appoint the company's first auditors or, if auditors resign mid year, they may appoint auditors to fill this 'casual vacancy' until the next AGM. |
| --- | --- |
| **Secretary of State for Business, Enterprise and Regulatory Reform** | May appoint auditors when the shareholders fail to reach an agreement. |

## 2.5 REMOVAL OF EXTERNAL AUDITORS

### 2.5.1 *RESIGNATION*

Sometimes it is necessary for the auditors to **resign**. If an auditor resigns, they should do so in writing and they may wish to speak to the shareholders to explain their reasons. The law gives the auditor two specific rights in this case:

- the right to send a **written explanation** to shareholders (a written representation); and
- the right to request a General Meeting where they may **speak** to the shareholders.

Once the auditors have resigned they must issue a **Statement of Circumstances**. This statement explains the specific reasons for the resignation or removal. Or, if there are no reasons, this too must be stated.

### 2.5.2 *FORCED REMOVAL*

Sometimes, the Board of Directors or some shareholders may wish to **remove** the auditors.

A General Meeting must be called so that the shareholders can vote on the proposal (via an ordinary resolution). Once again, the auditors have a legal right to send a written explanation to the shareholders or speak at the General Meeting.

Again, once the auditors have been removed, they must issue a Statement of Circumstances.

### 2.5.3 *AUDITORS DO NOT WISH TO SEEK REAPPOINTMENT*

Sometimes the auditors finish the annual audit and decide they do not wish to audit the company in future years. As such, when the board asks them to accept nomination for the following year, the auditors should politely decline and issue a Statement of Circumstances

### **Rights and Responsibilities**

In this section, we look in some detail at the rights and responsibilities of the parties involved in the audit. Specifically, we consider:

- the regal rights and responsibilities of external auditors;
- the responsibilities of company directors; and
- rights and responsibilities with regards to fraud.

## 2.6 LEGAL RIGHTS AND RESPONSIBILITIES OF EXTERNAL AUDITORS

### 2.6.1 *RIGHTS*

Auditors are usually given rights within national law to help ensure they can do their job properly. Rights will vary between countries but typically include:

- The right to access all books and records of the company.
- Access to all information and explanations.

- The right to:
  - o receive notice of a general meeting;
  - o attend a general meeting;
  - o speak at a general meeting.
- the right to resign;
- the right to circulate information to shareholders.

### 2.6.2 RESPONSIBLITIES

Typically, auditor duties are also set by the national government so once again, will vary from country to country. Typical duties include:

- To audit the financial statements and give an opinion on:
  - o truth and Fairness;
  - o whether or not they are properly prepared (in accordance with national rules);
  - o any other opinion required by government e.g. whether proper accounting records have been kept or if the Director's report is consistent with the financial statements.
- to issue a **Statement of Circumstances** on resignation or removal from a client. This statement explains the specific reasons for the resignation or removal. Or, if there are no reasons, this is also stated;
- after leaving a client to respond to any requests for information from the new incoming auditors.

### 2.7 DIRECTOR RESPONSIBILITIES

Directors have overall responsibility for running the company on a day-to-day basis. As far as auditors are concerned, however, their primary responsibility is to:

- ***Produce Financial Statements showing a true and fair view.***

Other Secondary responsibilities:

- to keep adequate accounting records;
- to give the auditors reasonable explanations;
- to apply the accounting standards correctly;
- to select appropriate accounting policies;
- to appropriately apply the going concern basis of accounting;
- to design and implement appropriate accounting system;
- to implement internal controls to actively prevent and detect errors and fraud.

### 2.8 FRAUD

Many people assume that the auditors are there to primarily find company fraud, however, this is not the case. An external auditor's job is to give an opinion on the truth and fairness of the financial statements. Fraudulent financial reporting, however, is likely to have an effect on these financial statements. We consider the responsibilities of directors and auditors with regards to fraud by distinguishing between:

- fraud prevention; and
- fraud detection.

### 2.8.1 FRAUD PREVENTION

Fraud prevention is entirely the responsibility of directors.

The external auditor has no legal obligation to prevent fraud but has a professional obligation to advise clients on how best to prevent it.

### 2.8.2 FRAUD DETECTION

Fraud detection is also the responsibility of directors.

However, external auditors have some responsibility.

> The external auditors are expected to plan and carry out their work so as to have a reasonable expectation of detecting material misstatements due to fraud or error.

In other words the external auditor has a responsibility to try to detect material fraud.

### 2.9 OTHER PRE-ACCEPTANCE CONSIDERATIONS

Apart from the ethical and legal issues we have already covered, there are a number of other issues that audit firms should consider before accepting appointment. These can be conveniently split into two main areas:

- client assessment; and
- professional clearance.

### 2.10 CLIENT ASSESSMENT CONSIDERATIONS

- resources (time and staff) available to do the work;
- the fee and the client's credit rating;
- client deadlines;
- the integrity of the client and its directors;
- the level of audit risk;
- money Laundering procedures to verify the identity of the client and their source of income.

### 2.11 PROFESSIONAL CLEARANCE

It is imperative that the incoming auditors obtain professional clearance before accepting a new appointment. This is a rigorous process that involves contacting the client's previous auditors to discuss potential reasons why the appointment should not be accepted.

Often clients have perfectly good reasons for removing their previous auditors for example; the previous auditors were not providing value for money. What is unacceptable, however, is the client removing the auditors because they wrongly disagree with their audit opinion. This is known as **opinion shopping**. In contacting the outgoing auditors, the incoming auditors will be able to decide whether the client has a legitimate reason for changing auditors or is in fact opinion shopping.

The following flow-chart summarises the process.

**The Professional Clearance Flowchart**

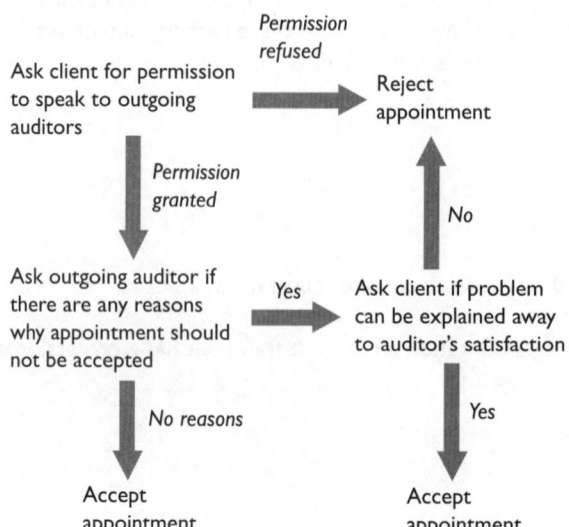

2.12    ACCEPTANCE OF A CLIENT AND ENGAGEMENT LETTERS

Assuming the above procedures have been followed, the incoming auditors are almost in a position to accept appointment.  Final considerations are:

- ensure resignation/removal and appointment of the outgoing and incoming auditors has been conducted in accordance with the legal requirements;
- create an **engagement letter** for the auditors and the client to sign.

2.13    ENGAGEMENT LETTERS

For any piece of work it is necessary to have a contract in place that sets out the terms of the assignment. A contract will

- reduce misunderstandings;
- create a legal basis for payment.

Audit work is no different and the auditors should ensure a contract, known here as an **Engagement Letter**, is signed immediately after appointment.

Engagement letters tend to have a standard format and content including:

- the objective and scope of the audit;
- responsibilities of directors and auditors;
- the nature of audit work i.e. testing;
- basis on which fees are calculated;
- the format of any reports that will be issued.

# Solution 1

## Jermain Ltd
### Ethical Threat

The audit partner of Miles & Co will have a close personal relationship with the finance director of Jermain (his brother) so therefore his objectivity and independence will be threatened.

If the audit partner comes across material errors in the financial statements he may be reluctant to issue a qualified opinion as this may affect his relationship with his brother.

Even if the partner and his brother do not have a close relationship the perception that they are close may still exist amongst outsiders.

### Safeguards

The only acceptable safeguard in this situation is for Miles & Co to resign as auditors of Jermain Ltd.

## Pebbles Beach Wear Ltd
### Ethical Threat

If the audit team manager helps the client to prepare its tax figure he will end up auditing this figure and therefore the self-review threat exists.

There is the risk that the team manager does not spot (or ignores) the errors in his own work.

We could also suggest that the management threat exists here.  Ultimately, the directors are responsible for the numbers in the Financial Statements so the auditors are taking on a management role if they carry out this task for them.

### Safeguards

In order to mitigate the self-review threat another member of Miles & Co staff, who is not involved in the audit, should help with the tax figures. The second partner should review the audit work on the tax figures. To mitigate the management threat we should ensure that the client accepts final responsibility for the numbers in the financial statements.

If we decide that the self-review and management threat are too great, even with the safeguards in place, then we should politely decline the tax work.

**Bingo UK Ltd**

**Ethical Threats**

With Bingo UK expanding so rapidly, Miles & Co we will have to consider whether or not they still have the resources as a firm to perform their audit competently.

Both preparing and auditing the Financial Statements gives rise to the self-review threat and although we have safeguards in place to mitigate this, once Bingo UK becomes listed we will not be able to perform this function anymore.

Also, when Bingo lists, the maximum fee we can receive from them will fall from 15% to 10% of our firm's total income. We are therefore at risk of breaching the fee limit and which may be perceived as a threat to our independence.

**Safeguards**

Miles & Co will need to show that they have the necessary resources to service a larger client.

Once Bingo lists, Miles & Co will need to politely refuse to prepare the Financial Statements.

Miles & Co should regularly review their fees from clients to ensure that they do not breach the limits set by the ACCA's Code of Conduct. If Bingo's listing results in the fee limit being breached they may need to consider resigning as auditors.

## Learning Summary

- Watch the video clip on audit ethics.
- Without referring to your notes, make sure you can describe the five ACCA ethical principles and the six threats to independence.
- Read the ACCA student article *Auditors and Fraud*.
- *http://www.accaglobal.com/students/publications/student_accountant/archive/2009/94/3190975*

3

Planning

# Context

Any project that is not planned effectively risks going wrong at some point. The worst possible outcome for the auditors would be to give the wrong opinion on the Financial Statements and to be subsequently sued by the shareholders. After accepting appointment, all auditors will plan the audit work. Effective planning ensures that the audit work is properly organised and managed, that the right people are assigned to the job and, most importantly, areas of audit risk are identified and dealt with. Audit risks are identified by auditors through careful consideration of all aspects of the clients' business and through the use of analytical procedures.

# Exam Hints

In June 2008 students were asked to define the term analytical procedures, describe different types of analytical procedures and state when they are used during the audit. They were then asked to use analytical procedures to identify and explain unusual items in a client's Income Statement.

In December 2008 students were asked to define the term 'audit risk' and then go on to spot inherent risks for a charity.

# Key Learning Points

- Planning ensures that audits are managed and organised properly, that the right amount and type of resources to are allocated to the job and that audit risk is kept to a minimum.
- Audit risk is the risk that the auditors give the wrong opinion on the Financial Statements.
- The audit risk model states that audit risk is made up of inherent, control and detection risks.
- Analytical procedures are used throughout the audit process: at the planning stage to help identify risk, at the evidence stage to help substantiate balances and at the completion stage as a final sense check of the financial statements.
- Something is material if it is important enough to affect the decisions of the users of Financial Statements. Its importance can be determined by its size or by its very nature.

# Chapter Overview

In this chapter we will cover the following aspects of the planning process:

- why auditors plan;
- understanding the audit client;
- audit risk;
- using analytical review to identify audit risk;
- we also revisit the concept of materiality.

# 3. Planning

### 3.1 WHY PLAN?

Unless you are very fortunate, any task that is not planned properly will probably go wrong! It could take too long, not address the key risks, or go over budget.

It is a key requirement of the ISAs that all audits are planned properly so that:

- auditors can determine the amount of work that needs to be done and therefore allocate the right amount and type of people to the job;
- the work is properly organised and managed;
- the correct fee can be determined;
- the work is carried out, within budget, and meets deadlines;
- important or problem areas are identified and dealt with appropriately so that auditors can identify and deal with **risk**.

Audit planning involves setting an **audit strategy** and, following on from this, a detailed **audit plan**.

### 3.1.1 *AUDIT STRATEGY*

For each audit client, an appropriate strategy needs to be considered. The strategy covers the **scope, timing** and **direction** of the audit. More specifically it will consider:

- the client's activities (and any changes to these activities since the previous year);
- their reporting framework (i.e. which accounting standards they follow);
- key reporting dates;
- the audit approach (controls or substantive testing);
- initial assessment of materiality;
- timing of the audit work;
- key audit risks.

### 3.1.2 *DETAILED AUDIT PLAN*

The audit plan is derived from the audit strategy. It is much more detailed than the strategy and includes a set of instructions to the audit team that set out many of the audit procedures. It is likely to include:

- A more detailed description of the client including:
  - o economic factors and industry conditions;
  - o financial performance;
  - o key changes in the business.
- A description of key accounting policies and internal control systems (including consideration of client's own internal audit department if applicable).
- A more detailed materiality assessment.
- Results of preliminary analytical procedures on the draft Financial Statements.
- Likely audit approach (controls or substantive) for each area of the Financial Statements.
- Detailed description of the high risk areas.
- Specific audit testing issues e.g:
  - o whether or not experts will be needed;
  - o use of computer assisted audit techniques (CAATS).
- Timing of specific procedures e.g. the stock-take.
- Details of staffing, a budget and a timetable.

## 3.2 UNDERSTANDING THE AUDIT CLIENT

It would be impossible to set the audit strategy, the detailed audit plan and assess the potential audit risks without first ensuring that the auditors have sufficient knowledge of the audit client. The ISA's make it clear that auditors need to **obtain an understanding of the audit client and it's environment.**

So, what do we need to know? Well in short, everything! Although the following diagram gives us some examples:

### 3.2.1 *UNDERSTANDING THE AUDIT CLIENT*

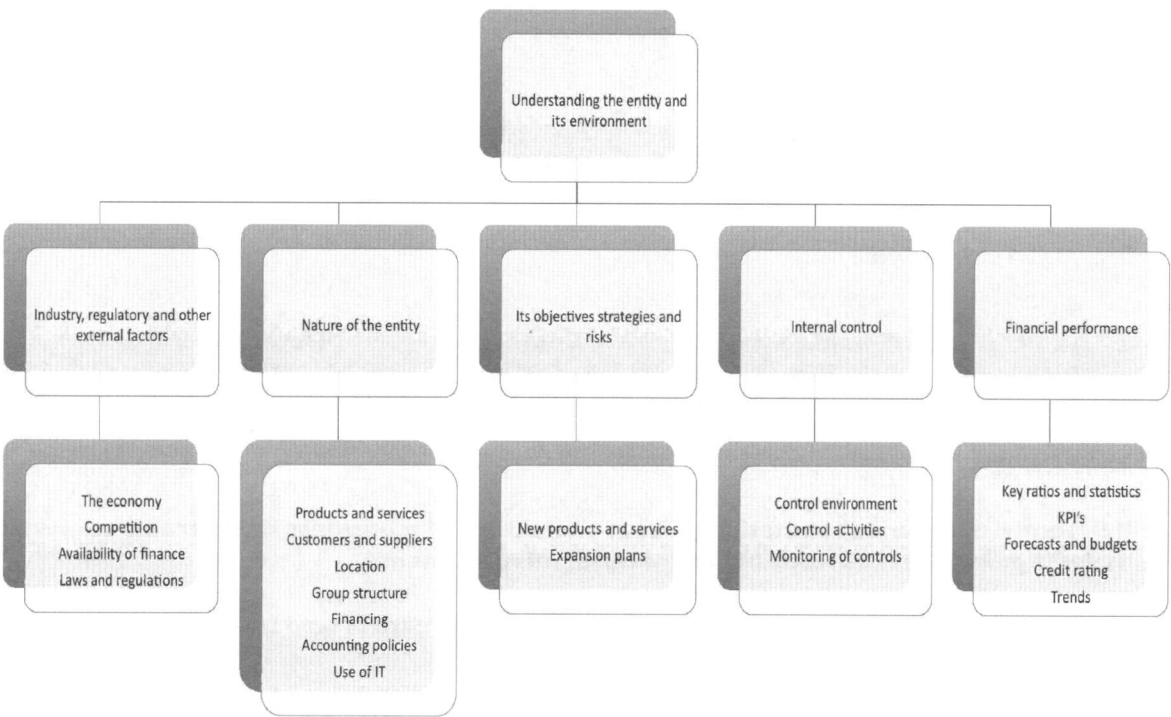

# Learning Example 1

For the last three years, your audit firm has been auditing Lowkey Ltd, a company specialising in event organisation. As part of the planning process, you are updating your knowledge of the client and its environment. Generate ideas as to where you will find the information you need.

## 3.3 AUDIT RISK – THE PRACTICAL ASPECTS

As we have seen, a hugely important part of the planning process is assessing **AUDIT RISK**.

### Definition

**<u>Audit risk</u> is the risk that the auditors give the <u>wrong opinion</u> on the financial statements**

This occurs if auditors sign off the financial statements as *true and fair* when in fact, they are *materially misstated* in some way.

Most commonly, this means that the auditors have failed to notice a material error in the numbers or disclosures, but it can also arise when the auditors sign off the financial statements as a going concern when in fact the company is (or very soon will be) bankrupt.

# Exam Tip

When you are asked to spot issues in a scenario that could give rise to audit risk you should look for:

- Things that could cause material errors;
- Things that risk the company's going concern status.

It is crucial that during planning auditors try to identify the areas of the financial statements that are at greatest risk of misstatement and devote appropriate attention to these areas. If risk is ignored and auditors give the wrong opinion then they can be sued by the shareholders.

### 3.4 AUDIT RISK – THE THEORY

Theoretically audit risk is said to result from the interaction of three different types of risk. This is illustrated by the **audit risk model.**

### 3.5 THE AUDIT RISK MODEL

| Audit Risk | = | Inherent Risk | x | Control Risk | x | Detection Risk |
|---|---|---|---|---|---|---|

#### 3.5.1 INHERENT RISK

**Inherent risk describes something about the nature of a business or its transactions that make it particularly susceptible to material misstatements.**

Examples of inherent risks for companies are limitless, however, here are a few examples:

- The car industry is one of the first industries to suffer during an economic downturn due to the reluctance of the population to spend money or take out loans that they may struggle to pay back. For this reason, we could say that the car industry is inherently risky.

- Financial institutions deal with complex financial instruments such as derivatives. These instruments can be incredibly difficult to account for and value and so are inherently risky.

- Companies such as Top Shop and Primark operate in the fashion industry where trends and tastes change rapidly. For companies such as these, sales and inventory balances are inherently risky.

- A company is heavily financed by debt. This is inherently risky as missed interest payments and repayments may lead to insolvency.

- A company operates a profit related bonus scheme. Its profit figures are inherently risky as there is the incentive to management to manipulate them to achieve the bonus targets.

#### 3.5.2 CONTROL RISK

If internal controls are the measures put in place by directors to help prevent and detect fraud and error then it follows that **control risk is the risk that a company's controls fail to prevent or detect material fraud or errors** (either because they don't exist, they are designed badly or they do not operate properly).

Examples of control risk are:

- bank reconciliations are not performed, so errors in the cash book may go undetected;
- expense claims are not authorised by a manager before they are paid so fraudulent claims go undetected.

Responsibility for mitigating inherent and control risks lies with company directors (although auditors may recommend improvements to internal controls).

### 3.5.3    DETECTION RISK

The final risk in the audit risk model is **detection risk**. Detection risk is all down to the auditors and is the **risk that the auditor's procedures fail to detect a material misstatement**. This could be due to a number of factors such as:

- choosing the wrong sample to test;
- human error;
- lack of training;
- inexperience.

### 3.6    INTERACTION OF THE AUDIT RISK MODEL

Audit risk should be *as low as possible* for every single client. As we have seen, auditors have very little control over inherent and control risk so they manage the overall risk by **manipulating detection risk** (the risk that they do have control over!).

**Let's see this in an illustration:**

An audit firm has two clients, A and B.

A Ltd operates in an industry that is highly exposed to the economic climate, uses lots of complex treasury instruments such as interest rate swaps and futures and has a very poor system of internal controls

B Ltd operates in a low risk industry, has few complex transactions and a highly sophisticated system of internal controls.

**A Ltd's Audit Risk Model**

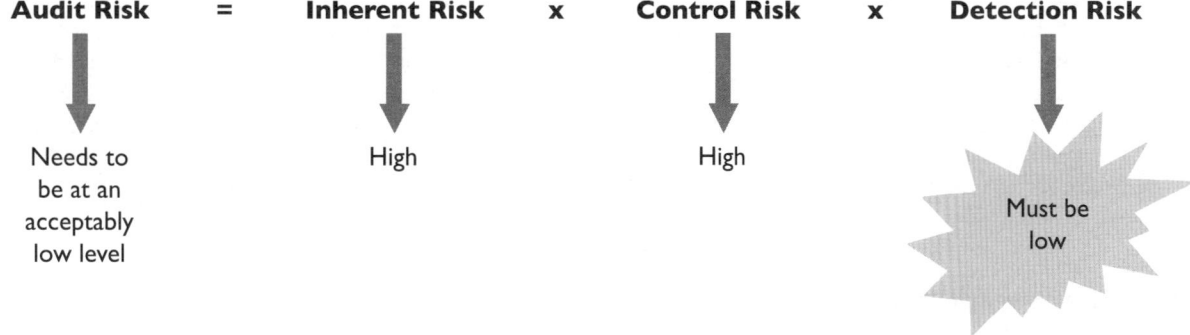

| **Audit Risk** | = | **Inherent Risk** | x | **Control Risk** | x | **Detection Risk** |

Needs to be at an acceptably low level | High | High | Must be low

As inherent risk and control risk are so high, the only way we can bring audit risk down to an acceptably low level is to lower detection risk. This means that the risk of the auditors not finding a misstatement needs to be low. In practice this means that the auditors need to do **more work**:

- less reliance on controls and more substantive testing;
- larger sample sizes;
- more experienced auditors.

**Remember to lower detection risk auditors need to do more work.**

**B Ltd's Audit Risk Model**

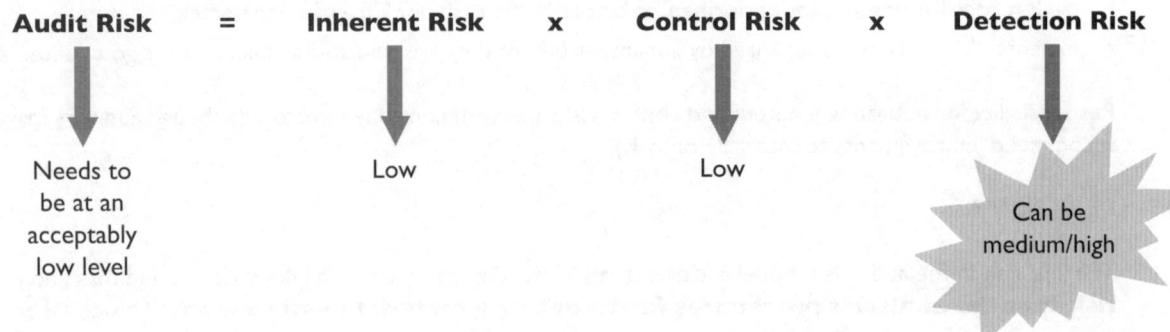

| Audit Risk | = | Inherent Risk | x | Control Risk | x | Detection Risk |
|---|---|---|---|---|---|---|
| Needs to be at an acceptably low level | | Low | | Low | | Can be medium/high |

As inherent and control risk are low then theoretically detection risk can afford to be high. Be careful, however, as this is a theoretical concept and under no circumstances will the auditors do no work! They can just do a different type of work:

More reliance on the strong internal controls and less detailed substantive testing.

# Learning Example 2

For each of the following clients determine the level of inherent and control risk. Then, using the audit risk model, determine what detection risk should be in order to reduce audit risk to an acceptably low level.

### Paws and Co

Paws and Co is an exclusive doggy day care centre, which provides wealthy dog owners with a number of services for their dogs. These services include dog sitting, dog walking and grooming. The owner of Paws and Co, Jo Whoof, set up the company 10 years ago after gaining her dog training qualification. The business was financed by her own personal wealth and there has been no need for any external finance. It has been performing well for the last 10 years. Jo has set up a very strong system of internal controls. She employs a qualified bookkeeper to prepare her financial statements and all dog handlers must have the necessary qualifications to work for her. Transactions are relatively straightforward and she has full liability insurance.

### Muttz

Muttz is a charity that takes in stray dogs and finds them to suitable new homes. Tess Leash founded it two years ago after she left her teaching post to do 'something worthwhile'. While waiting for adoption, the dogs are housed in kennels, which are rented from the local authority. The charity relies heavily on public donations for support. There is a team of five volunteer staff who run the charity on a day-to-day basis including looking after the dogs, dealing with donations and expenses and preparing the accounts. Tess is so busy with the dogs that she has not yet sorted out the public liability insurance she needs. Tess says she has no need for internal controls, as all of her volunteers are trustworthy.

## 3.7    ANALYTICAL PROCEDURES

Analytical procedures are a very important tool used by auditors.

They are used at many different stages throughout the audit:

| | |
|---|---|
| **At planning** | Here their use is compulsory to help identify risk. |
| **When gathering evidence** | To help to substantiate balances. |
| **At completion** | As a final sense check on the financial statements. |

When performing an **analytical procedure**, the auditor **compares** numbers, ratios or even non-financial information in order to identify unexpected trends or unexpected relationships, which may indicate the existence of errors.

There are many different analytical procedures including comparisons made of figures:

- year on year (e.g. revenue this year compared to revenue last year);
- to budget or forecast (e.g. actual purchases compared to budgeted purchases);
- to predictions made by the auditors (e.g. auditors calculation of depreciation compared to client's calculation);
- to industry information (e.g. client's revenue compared to competitor's revenue).

The results of these analytical procedures should be **investigated** and any findings **corroborated (confirmed)** with the auditor's knowledge of the business or external evidence. If there are any unexpected relationships, or results that do not make sense, then more detailed audit testing should be performed in these areas.

### Illustration of the Use of Analytical Procedures

Towards the end of the previous financial year, your client lost a customer that contributed 50% of their revenue for the year. You are now at the planning stage of this year's audit and have performed some analytical procedures on the Income Statement to identify potential risk areas.

You would expect, due to the loss of the customer, for revenue to be around about 50% lower than last year, however, your results tell you that revenue has increased by 10%. As this is so unexpected, you quite rightly think that revenue may be at risk of overstatement.

You **investigate** this unexpected result by asking the client why revenue has increased by 10%. The client responds by telling you that they have a new customer, which has replaced the old one.

Your work is not finished, however, and your next step is to **corroborate** this fact. You ask the client to show you the contract that was signed with the new customer and you trace a sample of their payments on account to the bank statement.

## 3.8 THE USE OF RATIOS DURING ANALYTICAL PROCEDURES

Calculating ratios is a very useful tool when performing analytical procedures.

In a set of Financial Statements, it is possible to divide almost any figure by almost any figure and come up with a percentage or ratio. The following six ratios however are the most important for the F8 examination.

# Learning Example 3

An auditor has been performing some analytical procedures at the planning stage of an audit. She has calculated a number of ratios using the draft financial statements (plus prior year comparatives) and has come up with the following results, which identify some potential audit risks that will need to be followed up. For each set of ratios, *identify what the potential audit risks could be*.

You have not been given any background information to help you so use your imagination! The first is done for you as an illustration.

**Gross Profit Margin**

This year        25.3%
Last year       11.2%

A significant increase in gross profit margin may suggest that:

* revenue is overstated e.g. by deliberately overstating the sales price;
* costs have been understated e.g. by deliberate non-recording of purchases or deferring some of this years costs to next year.

**Gearing**

This year        62%              Last year       34%

**ROCE**

This year        34%              Last year       22%

**Stock Days**

This year        98 days          Last year       42 days

**Debtor Days**

This year        63 days          Last year       34 days

## 3.9    MATERIALITY

When we looked at the basic principles of audit and assurance back in chapter 1, we saw that the objective of a statutory audit is to ensure that the Financial Statements are not **materially** misstated i.e. if the auditors will ask the client to adjust for material errors but will they ignore immaterial ones.

So, what do we mean by materiality?

**Something is *material* if it is important enough to affect the decisions of the users of Financial Statements.**

So how we define important? Well, there is no exact scientific definition so materiality is really a matter of **professional judgement** however there are some **guidelines**, which we find useful as auditors.

## 3.10 MATERIALITY GUIDELINES

Generally, something could be material in one of two ways:

| Quantatively |
| --- |
| • Something that is important due to its **size**<br><br>• As a guide, something is big enough to be material if it is *at least*:<br><br>• ½ - 1% of revenue;<br><br>• 1 – 2% of total assets; or<br><br>• 5 – 10% of PBT. |

| Quantatively |
| --- |
| • Something that is important due to its **nature.**<br><br>• These are items that are so important to the shareholders that they will not tolerate any error.<br><br>• Examples include director's pay and related party transactions. |

As mentioned before, it is important to understand that these are guidelines only. Different audit firms will have slightly different methods of calculating materiality.

## 3.11 OTHER ISSUES WITH MATERIALITY

Materiality is likely to be initially assessed at the planning or interim audit stage based upon results to date and forecast or budget results for the final few months. As a result, the initial assessment of materiality may change when the final audit is started and the draft financial statements are available. This materiality level must be constantly reviewed as the audit progresses. Further changes may be required due to:

* alterations to the draft accounts;
* changes in the assessment of control or audit risks;
* errors found in testing.

All immaterial errors should be noted down and added up at the end of the audit. It could be that several small errors add up to an overall material error!

# Solution to Learning Example 1

**Externally:**

- companies house records;
- prior year financial statements;
- newspapers;
- industry journals;
- internet search.

**From the Client:**

- visits to and meetings with the client;
- client brochures;
- client website;
- minutes of board meetings.

**From within the Audit Firm:**

- previous year audit files;
- audit team members.

# Solution to Learning Example 2

**Paws and Co**

*Inherent risk = Low*

The business is well established, performing well and has no need for external finance therefore is not exposed to fluctuating interest rates and the risk of non-repayment, which can lead to insolvency. All staff are fully qualified to perform their roles and there is full insurance should there be an incident with one of the dogs. There is a slight risk however that her business is not recession proof, if disposable incomes fall, dog owners may cut back on the amount of money they spend.

*Control risk = Low*

There is a strong system of internal controls and the bookkeeper is fully qualified therefore the risk of errors in the Financial Statements is reduced

*Detection risk*

Due to the low inherent and control risk, the detection risk can **medium/high**. The auditors of Paws and Co can focus on testing the internal controls and reduce the amount of substantive testing that they do.

**Muttz**

*Inherent risk = high*

This is a new charity that relies heavily on public donations. If the donations stop, the charity would quickly run out of money. Tess has not yet sorted out her public liability insurance so if there is an accident with a dog that leads to a court case a heavy fine or damages could wipe out the charity's income and severely damage its reputation.

*Control risk = high*

The system of internal controls is very weak, as Tess prefers to rely on trust. Tess has no prior experience of running a charity, plus her staff consists of five volunteers who are less likely to have the experience and qualifications of paid employees therefore the risk of errors in the accounts is high.

*Detection risk*

Detection risk for Muttz must be low. Inherent and control risk are high so there is a significant risk of material misstatement in the accounts. The auditors have no internal controls to rely on so there will be a lot of substantive testing needed.

## Solution to Learning Example 3

### Gearing

A significant increase in gearing suggests an increase in the company's levels of debt. More debt leads to increased interest payments, which will squeeze profit margins. Plus there is the risk of default in interest and capital repayments, which could lead to insolvency.

### ROCE

ROCE has increased which would suggest an increase in profit before interest and tax or a decrease in the company's resources (debt plus equity).

As gearing has increased significantly (therefore debt has increased), it would seem inconsistent that ROCE should increase. This could suggest that PBIT has been deliberately overstated.

### Stock Days

A significant increase in stock days could indicate:

- possible obsolescence leading to stock being overvalued;
- falling sales which could cast doubt over the company's going concern status.

### Debtor Days

An increase in debtor days could suggest potential risks such as:

- unreliable credit control procedures signifying a weak control environment overall;
- customers being unable to pay, leading to cash flow problems for the client and hence potential going concern problems.

## Learning Summary

- Ensure you can explain the terms audit risk, inherent risk, control risk and detection risk without reference to your notes.

- Watch the video clip 'planning'.

- Choose a well known company whose financial statements are available in the internet (it could be Marks & Spencer again) and calculate the six key ratios using its balance sheet and income statement.

- Read the ACCA student article 'The risk based approach to and audit and audit planning'.

- *http://www.accaglobal.com/students/publications/student_accountant/archive/2008/85/3086547*

London
School of Business
& Finance

shaping success in business and finance

# 4

## Introduction to Audit Evidence and Documentation

# Context

Once the auditors have planned the audit, they are then in a position to start gathering evidence in order to form their opinion on the Financial Statements. This evidence will come from a mixture of testing controls and the more detailed substantive testing. This chapter introduces some of the fundamental concepts of audit evidence, which will underpin any exam questions about detailed testing. It also covers some other areas such as relying on the work of experts, auditing accounting estimates and working papers. The detailed testing of specific financial statement balances is covered in later chapters.

# Exam Hints

The different types of audit test covered in this chapter will be crucial in helping you to answer the longer scenario question in the exam.

In December 2007 students were asked to explain the aim of a test of control, the aim of a substantive test and give an example of each.

In December 2008 students were asked to list the Financial Statement assertions over receivables and to give an example of an audit procedure to test each assertion.

In June 2008 students were asked to describe the factors that affect the sufficiency of audit evidence.

# Key Learning Points

- Audit evidence should be sufficient, relevant and reliable.
- Relevant audit evidence is evidence that helps to prove one of the Financial Statement assertions.
- In order to rely on the work of experts (e.g. lawyers, actuaries, valuation experts) auditors must consider their experience, qualifications and quality of their work.
- ISAs require for the entire audit process to be documented in working papers. These papers should be sufficiently detailed so that someone not involved in the audit can follow them and understand the conclusions reached.

# Chapter Overview

As mentioned in the context setting, this chapter will:

- introduce the fundamental ideas regarding audit evidence;
- consider the reliance of auditors on third part experts;
- discuss the audit of accounting estimates;
- discuss the importance and the content of working papers.

# 4. Introduction to Audit Evidence and Documentation

## 4.1 INTRODUCTION TO AUDIT EVIDENCE

In order to form their opinion on the financial statements, auditors must obtain suitable **audit evidence** in the form of tests of controls and substantive tests. According to the ISA's, this audit evidence should have certain **characteristics**. It should be:

- **sufficient;**
- **reliable; and**
- **relevant.**

### 4.1.1 *SUFFICIENCY*

Sufficiency is a measure of **quantity** i.e. auditors must obtain enough evidence to form their opinion. Sufficiency is affected by:

- **Risk** – The riskier an item is, the more evidence the auditors should obtain about that item;
- **Materiality** – The more material an item is, the more evidence the auditors should obtain;
- **Reliability** – The less reliable audit evidence is, the more of it is needed and vice versa.

### 4.1.2 *RELIABILITY*

To be useful, audit evidence must be reliable in terms of its **source** and its **nature**. The following generalisations about the reliability of audit evidence are useful.

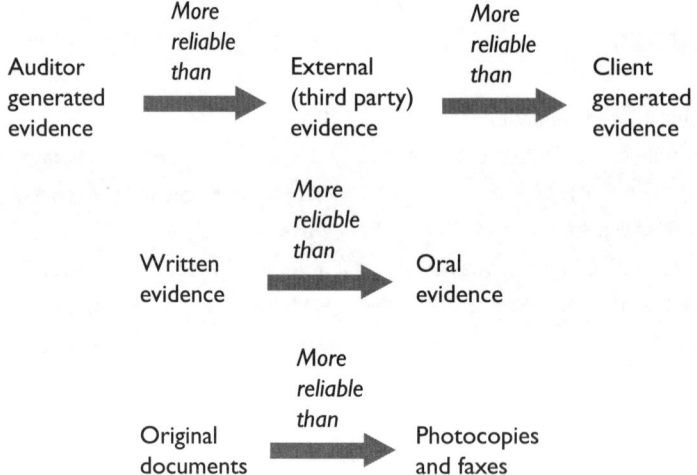

### 4.1.3 *RELEVANCE*

There are many reasons why the Financial Statements may have errors, deliberate or accidental, including things such as:

- transactions missed out;
- fake transactions recorded;
- transactions recorded at the wrong value;
- transactions recorded in the wrong accounting period.

As a result, the auditors must test a number of things **(assertions)** about each balance in the Financial Statements. These assertions are different depending upon whether you are testing a number in the Income Statement or a number in the Balance Sheet.

**Audit evidence is relevant if it tests one or more of these assertions.**

## 4.2 THE INCOME STATEMENT ASSERTIONS

The auditors must test the balances in the Income Statement for:

| Occurrence | Auditors must devise tests to ensure that the transactions in the Income Statement **actually took place** during that year. |
|---|---|
| Completeness | Auditors must devise tests to ensure that all of the transactions that took place during the year have actually **been recorded in the Income Statement.** |
| Accuracy | Auditors must devise tests to ensure that all of the transactions that took place during the year have **been recorded at the correct amounts.** |
| Cut off | Auditors must devise tests to ensure that the transactions that take place just before and just after the year end have **been recorded in the correct accounting period.** |
| Classification | Auditors must devise tests to ensure that the transactions have been recorded in the **correct account balances** e.g. interest payments recorded as 'finance costs' and not 'admin expenses'. |
| **Presentation and Disclosure** | Auditors must devise tests to ensure that the transactions have been presented and disclosed in accordance with the relevant financial reporting framework. |

## 4.3 THE BALANCE SHEET ASSERTIONS

The auditors must test items on the balance sheet for:

| Existence | Auditors must devise tests to ensure that the items on the Balance Sheet actually **exist** in real life. |
|---|---|
| Completeness | Auditors must devise tests to ensure that all of the items pertaining to the company (its assets, liabilities etc) have been **recorded on the balance sheet**. |
| **Rights and Obligations (OWNERSHIP)** | Auditors must devise tests to ensure that all of the assets on the balance sheet are **owned** by the company and all of the liabilities are an **obligation** of the company. |
| Valuation | Auditors must devise tests to ensure that the balances are recorded at the correct value. |
| **Presentation and Disclosure** | Auditors must devise tests to ensure that the transactions have been presented and disclosed in accordance with the relevant financial reporting framework. |

In the exam you will be asked to devise audit tests for certain items in the financial statements e.g. trade receivables, purchases, fixed assets. Use the assertions to help you generate ideas. To help you remember *some* of the assertions, you can use simple but effective mnemonic, **PROVE**.

**P** Presentation and Disclosure

**R** Records must be **accurate** and **complete**

**O** Ownership

**V** Valuation

**E** Existence

# Learning Example 1

> Your audit client is a large pharmaceutical company, which manufactures medicines. They employ a large sales team who travel around the country selling these products to GPs and hospitals. Each member of the sales team is provided with a company car, which has been acquired by the company on a finance lease. The audit team manager has asked you to devise a number of relevant audit tests to ensure that these cars are fairly stated on the balance sheet. Use the Financial Statement assertions to help you to generate ideas.

### 4.4 EVIDENCE GATHERING TECHNIQUES

In order to get obtain evidence, auditors can use a number of techniques. These are best remembered using the mnemonic AEIOU:

- **A**nalytical procedures (i.e. making comparisons and following up unexpected relationships).
- **E**nquiry and confirmation (asking questions of management and confirming their answers with other sources of evidence).
- **I**nspection (looking at the detail on invoices, ledgers etc).
- **O**bservation (watching employees perform their roles).
- Comp**U**tation (recalculation of the clients numbers to see if they are correct).

### 4.5 RELIANCE ON THE WORK OF THIRD PARTIES

In certain cases, auditors may rely on the work of **third parties** when gathering their audit evidence.

- Experts such as:
  - o lawyers;
  - o valuation experts;
  - o actuaries.
- The client's internal auditors (who have reviewed the internal controls).
- Another firm of external auditors (who may for example be auditing an overseas subsidiary of our client).

The external auditor retains full responsibility for the opinion, so when using the work of others it is essential to make sure that their work is reliable:

- Are they suitably **qualified**?
- Do they have the **experience**?
- Are they **independent** of the client?
- Did they carry out their work in a **professional** manner, planning and documenting their process and following professional standards?

### 4.6 THE AUDIT OF ACCOUNTING ESTIMATES

The financial statements of a company are full of estimates:

- doubtful debt provisions;
- depreciation;
- net realisable value;
- legal provisions.

Estimates are a particularly difficult area for the audit as they involve **considerable judgement** and are based upon **future events**. As a result, they are **easy to manipulate** so require particular attention.

There is some guidance in the ISAs to help auditors to audit accounting estimates:

| Review and test the process used by management to develop the estimate | For example:<br>• Enquire as to who determines the bad debt provision. – is it someone with seniority and experience?<br>• Assess whether provision has been accurate in the past.<br>• Recalculate the provision and compare it to client's figures. |
|---|---|
| Use an independent estimate for comparison | For example:<br>• Compare client's provision for legal costs to the independent estimate provided by the company solicitors. |
| Review subsequent events to assess reasonableness of the estimate made | For example:<br>• Compare the bad debt provision to the actual figure for bad debts after the year end. Was the provision adequate? |

## 4.7 AUDIT DOCUMENTATION

### 4.7.1 THE IMPORTANCE OF DOCUMENTATION

It is essential that the entire audit process be **documented** in working papers. The ISA's require that all audit working papers should be sufficiently **complete and detailed** in order to enable an experienced auditor with no previous connection with the audit to ascertain what work was performed to support the conclusions reached.

The benefits of such working papers are:

- the documents show that the audit work has been done properly and provide written evidence of the reasons for the auditor's conclusions should the audit opinion be called into question at a later date (e.g. in court);
- they enable senior staff to review the work of junior staff;
- they encourage a more methodical and rigorous approach;
- they assist the audit team in future years.

### 4.7.2 CONTENT OF WORKING PAPERS

The exact content of the working papers will depend upon the nature of the work being performed and the size and complexity of the client. The essential content for every working paper is illustrated below:

| Client | Zafiro Gems Ltd | Reference B/2/1 |
|---|---|---|
| | | Working paper reference |
| **Accounting Year End** | 31 December 2008 | |
| **Prepared by**<br>**Date** | M Bassett<br>27 February 2009 | |
| **Subject** | Review of bank reconciliations | |
| **Aim of the Work** | | |
| | The objective of the test | |
| **Work Done** | | |
| | Procedures performed<br>Sample chosen<br>Key audit risks addressed<br>Cross-referencing | |

London
School of Business
& Finance

shaping success in business and finance

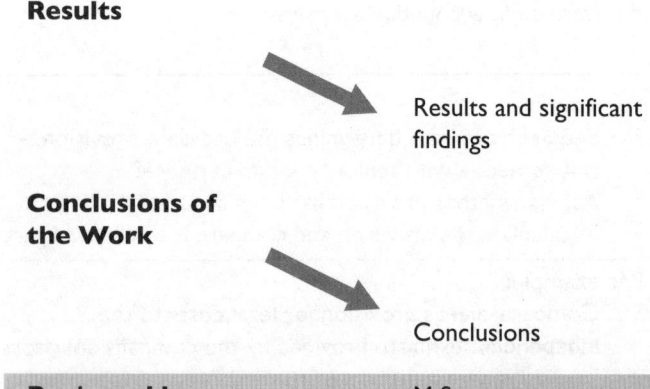

**Results**

Results and significant findings

**Conclusions of the Work**

Conclusions

| **Reviewed by** | M Smart |
|---|---|
| **Date of Review** | 3 March 2009 |

## 4.8 CURRENT AND PERMANENT AUDIT FILES

### 4.8.1 *CURRENT AUDIT FILES*

For each annual audit assignment, the working papers will be collected together in the **current audit file**. The file will show all of the work that was done throughout the audit process. There will be:

- a planning section;
- sections for each area of the financial statements showing what work was done.
- a completion section showing the final tasks carried out at the end of the audit including:
  - o a schedule of points for manager and partner attention;
  - o a schedule of points for next year's audit.

### 4.8.2 *PERMANENT AUDIT FILES*

There is some information that will be of use to continuing use to the audit year-on-year. This information is kept on the permanent file and includes items such as:

- the engagement letter;
- organisational charts showing group structure and key employees;
- systems flow charts;
- company Articles and Memorandum;
- long term agreements (e.g. loan agreements, finance lease agreements).

## 5.9 STANDARDISED AUDIT PROCEDURES

These are essentially pre-determined lists of tests for each area of the audit e.g. standard tests for non-current assets and standard tests for inventory etc. There are benefits and disadvantages to standardisation

| **Benefits** | <ul><li>Much easier to prepare and review procedures.</li><li>Can help in training junior staff.</li><li>Prompts auditor to think of and perform the right tests.</li><li>Quicker and more efficient as auditors do not have to devise their own tests for each audit.</li><li>Helps to ensure quality.</li></ul> |
|---|---|
| **Disadvantages** | <ul><li>No incentive for auditors to think for themselves.</li><li>Are not tailored to client therefore may not address specific risks.</li><li>If they are not updated, any mistakes will carry over each year to each audit.</li></ul> |

# Exam Question:  Delphic

Delphic is a wholesaler of furniture (such as chairs, tables and cupboards).  Delphic sells to over 600 customers ranging from large retail stores to smaller owner managed businesses. The receivables balances therefore range from $5,000 to $125,000.

**Required**

Explain the audit procedures that should be carried out on the trade receivables balance at Delphic, explaining the reason for each procedure.

**10 Marks**

# Exam Question:  Working Papers

It has been recommended that audit working papers should always be sufficiently complete and detailed to enable an experienced auditor with no previous connection with the audit to ascertain what work was performed to support the conclusions reached.

**Required**

a)  Describe four benefits that the auditor will obtain from producing working papers that meet the above requirement.

**4 marks**

b)  Describe four different review procedures that are applied to working papers.

**4 marks**

c)  Discuss the reliability of the following types of audit evidence, giving two examples of each form of evidence:

- evidence originated by the auditor;
- evidence created by third parties;
- evidence created by the management of the client.

**3 marks**

d)  Describe what evidence should be recorded in the current audit file when auditing a legal provision. Give reasons for the inclusion of such evidence.

**5 marks**

e)  Briefly explain the purpose of the Permanent Audit File.  List three types of information contained in the permanent audit file and the reasons for its inclusion.

**3 marks**

f)  Briefly explain the purpose (advantages) of standardised procedures.

**2 marks**

**20 Marks**

## Solution to Learning Example 1

| | |
|---|---|
| **Existence** | Select a sample of the cars from the fixed-asset register and go out to the car park and physically verify that they exist. |
| **Completeness** | Inspect a sample of the finance lease agreements and trace the details to the accounting records to ensure that both the relevant car is included the PPE register and the relevant finance lease creditor has been recorded in the creditors ledger. |
| **Rights and Obligations** | Inspect a sample of car lease agreements to ensure that the terms and conditions are those of a finance lease and therefore the company can show the cars on the fixed asset register. If there are any operating lease agreements, these cars should not be on the fixed asset register. |
| **Valuation** | Recalculate the depreciation on finance lease cars and compare to the client's depreciation to ensure that the net book value of the cars is appropriate. |
| **Presentation and Disclosure** | Review the balance of finance leased cars on the face of the balance sheet to ensure it has been presented net of depreciation. Review the finance lease creditor note to ensure the creditor balance has been split between current and non-current liabilities. |

**Remember, you can use PROVE to help you to remember some of the relevant assertions**

## Exam Question Debrief: Delphic

This is very typical of an evidence-style question. The examiner will give you a Financial Statement balance and expect you to generate audit procedures to test that balance.

There are 10 marks so you should be looking for 10 tests.

In these questions use your mnemonics to help you. You want to test the assertions that are relevant to trade receivables so use **'PROVE'**. This will give you five tests. Using the audit techniques from **AEIOU** should give you another five!

London
School of Business
& Finance

shaping success in business and finance

| **P**resentation and Disclosure | • Review the balance of trade receivables on the Balance Sheet to ensure that it is presented in accordance with the relevant reporting requirements i.e. trade receivables less bad debt provision. |
|---|---|
| **R**ecords <br> • Completeness <br><br> • Accuracy | • Review the receivables list for credit balances to be moved into creditors. <br> • Cast the receivables list to ensure that the total is accurate. |
| **O**wnership | • Trace a sample of receivable balances to the relevant sales invoice. <br> • Check the selling company name on the invoice to ensure that the debtors belong to the company. |
| **V**aluation | • Obtain the aged debtors analysis and trace old debts to the bad debt provision to ensure that they have been provided for. |
| **E**xistence | • Send a debtors' circularisation to confirm the existence of the receivables. |
| **A**nalytical review | • Calculate debtor days for each month of the year to ensure there are no unusual movements. An increase in debtor days may cast doubt on the recoverability of certain debts. |
| **E**nquiry | • Ask the receivables clerk about any problem customers and corroborate findings with customer payment history. Trace these balances to the bad debt provision to ensure they have been provided for. |
| **I**nspection | • Inspect and re-perform the receivables ledger control account reconciliation to ensure that the receivables list agrees to the receivables ledger. |
| **O**bservation | • Attend a meeting between the client and its major customer to assess the relationship. If the client loses the customer the going concern status may be threatened. |
| Comp**U**tation | • Select a sample of sales invoices and recalculate the sales tax to ensure its accuracy. |

# Exam Question Debrief: Working Papers

This is mostly a knowledge-based question with lots of easy marks available if you take the time to learn the basic points with regards to working papers, review and audit files. The tricky part of the question is part (d) where you have to say what evidence you would have on file when auditing a provision. Go back to the earlier part of the chapter and look at the guidance provided by the ISAs for auditing provisions to help you to generate ideas.

a) Four benefits of producing audit working papers are:

1. It ensures compliance with the ISAs so auditors can be seen to be following the professional standards.

2. Documenting work encourages a methodical and rigorous approach and hence helps to maintain quality.

3. Documentation of work enables review.

4. They provide written evidence of the work performed and the conclusions reached should the auditors opinion be called into question at a later date (e.g. during a court case).

b) The four different types of review procedure performed on working papers are:

1. *Hot review:* This is a review of the working papers by the audit supervisor prior to the audit report being signed. The purpose of this is to spot any mistakes in the audit process before the report is signed.

2. *Cold review:* This is where one office checks the working papers of another office within the same audit firm after the audit report has been signed. The purpose of this is to provide feedback and recommendations for improvement.

3. *Peer review:* This is where one small audit firm checks the working papers of another small audit firm (which does not have a second office to carry out cold review). Once again, this is to provide feedback and recommendations for improvement.

4. *Monitoring Unit review:* This is where a Recognised Supervisory Body (ACCA) review audit work on a sample basis.

c) Sources of evidence:

a. Auditor generated evidence is generally very reliable. Two examples are:
   i. auditor counts stock;
   ii. auditor recalculates depreciation.

b. External (third party) evidence is generally reliable. Two examples are:
   i. customer response to receivables circularisation;
   ii. bank statement to confirm bank balance.

c. Internal evidence (client generated) is not as reliable and needs corroboration. Two examples are:
   i. figures in the receivables ledger control account (or any client documentation);
   ii. any verbal explanation from the directors in response to an audit query.

d) Take care here. The question does not ask for **procedures** it asks for **evidence**. You should therefore be mentioning the **documents** you will be testing and why you are testing them.

The evidence you may have on file when auditing a legal provision:

- a schedule detailing prior year audit provisions so you can compare this year's to assess reasonableness;
- details of conversations with directors as to how they calculated the provision, the seniority of the person who did it and whether or not the provision has been reviewed by management;
- a copy of the lawyer's/solicitor's report detailing the expected damages so the provision can be compared to these;
- a copy of correspondence from the litigant to prove that our client has an obligation to them;
- any correspondence from the lawyers/courts after the year end to see if the case has been settled and if our provision was adequate.

e) Purpose of a permanent audit file

The permanent audit file collects information that is of **continuing** use to the audit year-on-year.

| Content | Purpose |
| --- | --- |
| • Engagement letter | To provide the terms of engagement which sets out scope and responsibilities |
| • Organisational chart | To provide the names of client management and key contacts |
| • Systems flow charts | To provide a reminder of how the systems operate and to form a basis for this year's tests of control |

f) Purpose (i.e. benefits) of standardised procedures

Standardised procedures are essentially a list of audit tests for each area of audit. Benefits of these standardised procedures are:

- they make delegation and training easier;
- they prompt the auditor to think of and perform the right tests in each area.

# Learning Summary

- Watch the video clip 'audit evidence'.
- Attempt the following exam standard questions 'Delphic' and 'Working papers'.
- Read the ACCA student article 'Working papers'.
- **http://www.accaglobal.com/students/publications/student_accountant/archive/2007/73/2883860**

# 5

# Assessing an Internal Control System

London
School of Business
& Finance

shaping success in business and finance

# Context

In order to determine their audit approach, auditors need to understand, document and evaluate their client's internal controls. The internal controls are primarily the measures put in place to prevent and detect error within a client's accounting systems. If controls are deemed to be weak, then more detailed substantive testing will need to be carried out on the balances in the Financial Statements. If controls are deemed to be strong, then the auditor can place reliance on those controls and reduce the amount of detailed testing.

# Exam Hints

Internal controls are a huge area of the syllabus and are therefore guaranteed to appear in some format in the exam.

The questions are most likely to be practical in nature. In December 2007 students were asked to identify weaknesses in a petty cash system and suggest ways these weaknesses could be overcome. In December 2008 students were asked to identify weaknesses in a wages system and suggest relevant controls.

# Key Learning Points

- Internal controls are primarily measures in place in accounting systems that help to prevent and detect fraud and error.
- The strength of the client's internal control systems determines the audit approach.
- Auditors evaluate a company's internal controls using Internal Control Questionnaires (ICQs) or Internal Control Evaluation Questionnaires (ICEQs).
- The auditor tests the internal controls to ensure they have been operating as described throughout the year.
- Weaknesses in internal controls are reported to directors in the management letter.

# Chapter Overview

This chapter introduces us to internal controls and in particular:

- the importance of internal controls;
- the components of an internal control system;
- how auditors assess internal controls;
- how auditors report weaknesses in controls to the directors.

# 5. Assessing an Internal Control System

## 5.1 THE IMPORTANCE OF INTERNAL CONTROLS

Internal control systems are the measures put in place by the directors of the company primarily to help **prevent and detect errors** in the recording of transactions. In addition internal controls should also exist to:

*   help to prevent and detect fraud;
*   help to safeguard assets;
*   ensure the business runs efficiently.

Auditors must assess and understand the internal control systems of their clients in order to determine their audit approach.

*   If the internal controls systems are strong then auditors can rely on these controls and reduce the amount of detailed (substantive) testing that they do.

*   If the internal controls systems are weak, the auditors cannot rely on these controls and must increase the amount of detailed (substantive) testing that they do.

## Learning Example 1

Before you move on spend 10 minutes and generate as many ideas as you can for the types of controls you may find in operation in a corner shop, using the above definitions of a control to help.

## 5.2 THE COMPONENTS OF AN INTERNAL CONTROL SYSTEM

It is generally accepted that a strong internal control system is made up of five elements:

1.  A strong **control environment;**
2.  Strong **control procedures;**
3.  Good **risk assessment;**
4.  Good **information systems;**
5.  Effective **monitoring** of the controls.

Let us look at each of these elements in turn.

## 5.3 CONTROL ENVIRONMENT

Controls are unlikely to be effective unless there is a strong control environment.

### Definition

**Control Environment** - The control environment includes the governance and management functions and the attitudes, awareness and actions of those charged with governance and management concerning the entity's internal control and its importance in the entity.

In less technical terms, the control environment considers, amongst other things:

| Management Attitude | • For the controls to be taken seriously in the organisation, the directors and management should show the right attitude.<br>• Lead by example by following the same controls as the staff and not overriding the controls.<br>• Discipline employees who breach controls. |
|---|---|
| Staff | • Must be trained and motivated to follow the controls.<br>• The recruitment process must aim to employ the right sort of people; those with discipline and willingness to understand the company and adhere to its policies. |
| Segregation of Duties | • Different parts of a transaction process should be shared by different employees.<br>• No employee should review their own work.<br>• No employee should have control over all elements of a transaction. |

## 5.4 CONTROL PROCEDURES

The control procedures are the actual *activities* that are carried out within the system to prevent and detect errors. These activities can be grouped into categories:

| **C**omparison Controls | Comparisons are a very powerful control. Imagine we budgeted to spend $1m on capital expenditure this year but the actual spend was $2m. This could suggest a number of issues:<br>• perhaps the 'actual' figure is wrong;<br>• perhaps the budgeting process is inadequate;<br>• perhaps there was no authorisation for the extra $1m. |
|---|---|
| **A**uthorisation | An appropriate person should approve transactions. For example, employee expense claims should be approved by a department manager to ensure no fraudulent expenses are being claimed. |
| **R**econciliations | A bank reconciliation can help to pick up errors between postings in the cash book and the bank statemen.t |
| **C**omputer Controls | Controls over access to computer systems, such as passwords, can help to prevent unauthorised access to books and records. |
| **A**rithmetical Controls | Checking to see if balances have been added up correctly or if number sequences are complete to detect missing transactions. |
| **P**hysical Controls | Physical controls such as CCTV, safes and locks can help to prevent theft and unauthorised access. |
| **S**egregation of Duties | Allocating tasks within an accounting system to different employees reduces the risk of fraud and makes the detection of errors more likely. |

You can use the mnemonic **CARCAPS** to help you to remember the types of activities. In the exam you will be asked to generate ideas for internal control activities in response to weaknesses in a system.

## 5.5 RISK ASSESSMENT

In order to design controls that will effectively prevent and detect errors within a system, directors must fully understand the risks that threaten the system in the first place.

For example, if directors do not understand that cash is at high risk of being stolen, they may not implement controls such as bank reconciliations, regular banking of excess cash and safe storage of petty cash.

Unfortunately, however, no internal control system can ever be 100% effective due to inherent weaknesses such as human error, override and possible collusion to commit fraud.

## 5.6 INFORMATION SYSTEMS

An information system consists of the procedures and records established to initiate, record and process a company's transactions. The internal controls will operate within these systems.

## 5.7 MONITORING

Sometimes controls that directors think are designed and working effectively can be out of date and often ignored by employees. Directors of companies should ensure that controls are monitored continually to ensure that they are being followed and achieving their objectives.

If the company has an Internal Audit department, they will carry out this monitoring role.

## 5.8 LIMITATIONS OF INTERNAL CONTROL SYSTEMS

As mentioned briefly earlier, no system of internal controls is ever 100% effective. Reasons for this include:

- human error;
- collusion to commit fraud;
- potential for management override;
- the cost/time to implement the controls may outweigh the benefit of following them so the controls are ignored;
- it may be impossible to design a control for a one-off transaction e.g. determining a provision for a court case. Controls work best in systems where there is a high volume of routine transactions.

It is for these reasons that the auditors will never perform a wholly controls based audit. **There will always be some element of substantive testing regardless of the strength of the controls systems.**

## 5.9 ASSESSING AN INTERNAL CONTROL SYSTEM

We now understand what internal controls are and what internal controls systems are consist of. Let us now look at how auditors go about assessing the system in order to decide whether to place reliance on it or not.

Auditors must **understand, document** and **evaluate** the client's internal control systems. If the controls appear to be strong at this point they are **tested** to ensure they operated throughout the financial year.

London
School of Business
& Finance

shaping success in business and finance

| Understand | • Auditors need to understand exactly how the system works. This is done via a **walkthrough** test i.e. following one transaction through the system from start to finish |
|---|---|

| Document | • Auditors need to document exactly how the system works. There are two ways of recording a system:<br><br>• **Narrative notes** i.e. write down the system using words<br><br>• **Flowcharts** |
|---|---|

| Evaluate | • There are three ways of evaluating a system:<br><br>• **Common sense** – it is often easy to tell when a system is weak. Obvious controls will be missing.<br><br>• **Internal Control Questionnaires** (ICQs) These are designed to ask if certain controls are present. E.g. 'are bank reconciliations performed monthly?'<br><br>• **Internal Control Evaluation Questionnaires** (ICEQs). These are designed to ask if certain errors can be prevented. E.g.' can cash be stolen?' |
|---|---|

| Test | • If the controls appear strong they are tested to ensure that they operated as described throughout the year.<br>•<br>• If the controls did operate effectively throughout the year the amount of substantive testing can be reduced |
|---|---|

## 5.10  REPORTING CONTROL WEAKNESSES TO THE CLIENT

If the auditor believes the controls could be improved, it is a matter of professional courtesy to advise the client of these weaknesses, the possible consequences of these weaknesses and recommendations for ways in which the controls could be improved.

This is done via the **management letter**, which is sent to the client after the controls testing or at the end of the audit.

The management letter has two parts:

1.  a covering letter;
2.  an appendix.

The covering letter is a brief note including:

- an explanation as to why the letter is being sent;
- a disclaimer saying that auditors have not necessarily spotted every weakness;
- a statement that the letter is for internal use only and not to be shared with third parties.

The appendix details:

- the weaknesses;
- the consequences;
- recommendations for improvement to the controls.

### 5.10.1 *MANAGEMENT LETTER ILLUSTRATION*

The Board of Directors
Capulina Ltd
1 High Street
London

DATE

Dear Sir/Madam

During the course of our audit of the company's financial statements for the year ended 31 December 2008, we examined the principal internal controls which the company has established to ensure the accuracy and reliability of its accounting records.

Reason we are writing

We are writing to draw your attention to the weaknesses discovered and to suggest ways in which the systems could be improved.

Disclaimer

Our examination is carried out for the purposes of our audit and does not necessarily disclose every weakness.

Please be aware that:

Report not to be used by third parties

This report is issued solely for the use of Capulina Ltd, it must not be disclosed to a third party. We assume no responsibility to any other person in connection with this report.

We thank your staff for their assistance during the audit.

We would be grateful if you would reply to the letter indicting your intended or actual action in respect of the items below.

Yours faithfully

*Smith and Co Chartered Accountants*

**Appendix**

| Weakness | Consequence | Recommendation |
|---|---|---|
| When goods arrive they are not checked to ensure that they are the goods that were ordered nor are they checked for quality. | • Company may accept and pay for for goods that were not ordered.<br>• Poor quality materials may lead to increased waste during production and poor quality products being sold on to customers which will damage the company's reputation purchase order before being accepted. | • When goods arrive a sample should be checked against agreed quality criteria.<br>• Agree a returns period with supplier to ensure time can be taken to check the goods properly.<br>• Goods received should be checked back to the approved purchase. |

5.11    THE AUDIT APPROACH: IT'S STARTING TO COME TOGETHER

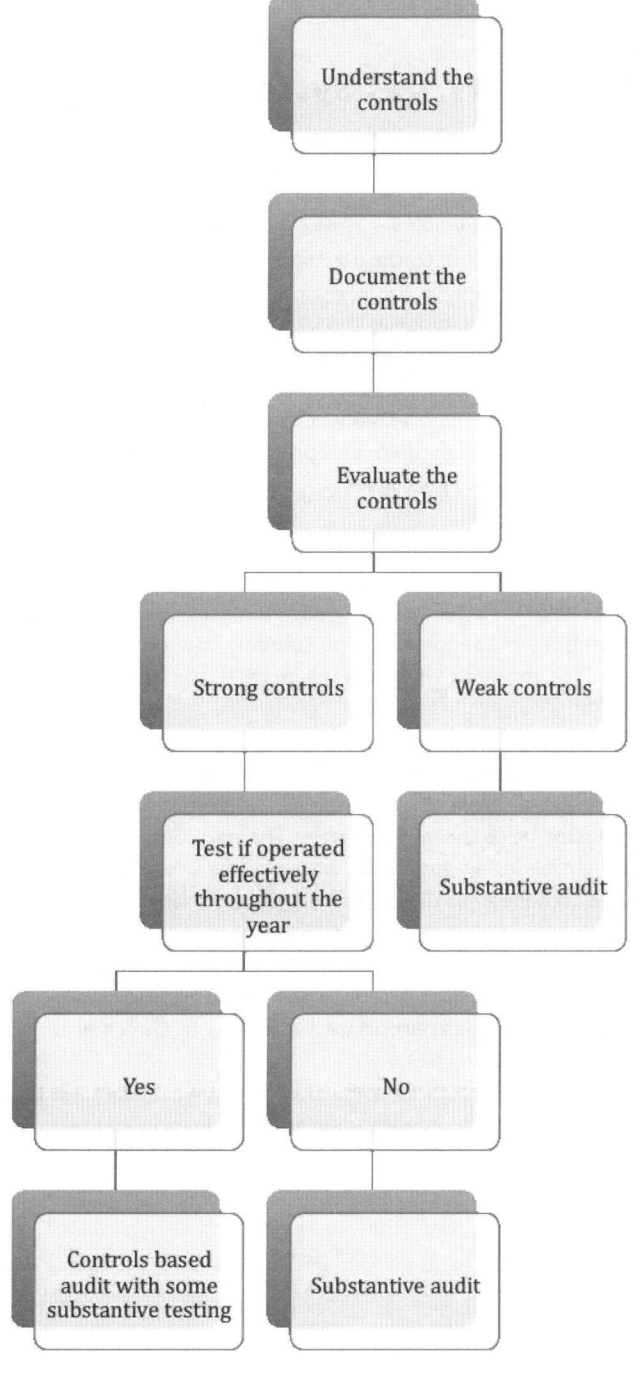

# Exam Question: Methods

Describe the methods which an auditor may use to record, ascertain and evaluate a system and how the results of the initial evaluation may be fed back to management.

**7 marks**

# Exam Question: Low Cost Supermarkets

As part of your audit of a low cost supermarket chain, you are in the process of determining an audit approach to the following two areas:

1. Bank          Two bank accounts, full reconciliations, complex system.
2. Purchases     Thousands of transactions, well controlled system.

**Required**

Compare the alternative audit approaches and select the best for each area

**4 marks**

# Exam Question: Burden (Wages System)

Burden manufactures a range of components and spare parts for the textile industry. The company employs 150 hourly-paid production workers and 90 selling, distributing and administrative staff, including the three directors of the company. There are two wages clerks who deal with the weekly payroll of the hourly-paid employees. They are directly responsible to the assistant accountant.

The company uses a computerised time clock at the factory gate to record the hours worked by the production employees. Each employee has a card with a magnetic strip with his own identification code on it. This card is inserted in the computerised time clock on the arrival and departure of the workers whereupon it records the hours worked on the card. The cards are collected weekly by the wages clerks who simply insert them individually into the microcomputer which then reads them and prepares the payroll. The production manager keeps the unused clock cards in a locked cabinet in his office.

Wages are paid one week in arrears. The wages clerks compile the payroll by means of the microcomputer system, pass the payroll to the assistant accountant who scrutinises it before drawing the wages cheque, which is passed to one of the directors for signature. Any pay increases are negotiated locally by representatives of the employees. If any alterations are required to the standing data on the microcomputer, then the wages clerks amend the records. For example, when a wage increase has been negotiated, the rates of pay are changed by the wages clerks.

The cheque is drawn to cover net wages and the cashier makes arrangements for collecting the cash from the bank. The wages clerks then make up the wages envelopes. Whenever there is assistance required on preparing wages, the assistant accountant helps the wages clerks. The payment of wages is carried out by the production manager who returns any unclaimed wages to the wages clerks who keep them in a locked filing cabinet. Each employee is expected to collect his unclaimed wages personally.

New production employees are notified to the wages department verbally by the production manager and when employees leave a note to that effect is sent to the wages department by the production manager. All statutory deductions are paid to the appropriate authorities by the chief accountant.

You have recently been appointed the auditor of Burden for the year ended 31 December and have just started your interim audit. You are about to commence your audit evaluation and testing of the wages system.

London
School of Business
& Finance

shaping success in business and finance

**Required**

(a) Describe the weaknesses in the present wages and salaries system, and suggest, with reasons, improvements which could be made to the system (assuming that the only controls are those set out above).

(18 marks)

(b) Describe the appropriate audit approach to wages, based on the above.

(2 marks)

**(20 marks)**

## Solution to Learning Example 1

The types of controls you may find in a corner shop include the following:

- CCTV over the till to help prevent theft;
- high value goods kept behind the till;
- cash banked regularly rather than keeping it on premises;
- reconciliation of till roll to takings;
- regular stock takes;
- regular bank reconciliation, reviewed by manager;
- purchases authorised by manager before order being placed;
- check stock levels before ordering to prevent over-ordering;
- check quantity and quality of deliveries before accepting;
- matching of purchase orders to delivery documents to ensure orders received.

## Exam Question Debrief: Methods

This is a knowledge-based question. You should be happy with how auditors come to understand client systems, the methods they use to document them and evaluate them and how the results are communicated to management.

You will produce a well-focused answer using four headings taken straight from the requirement:

1. Record.
2. Ascertain.
3. Evaluate.
4. Feedback to management.

(18 marks)

Describe the appropriate audit approach to wages, based on the above.

(2 marks)

**(20 marks)**

## Exam Question Debrief: Low Cost Supermarkets

### Bank Accounts

This complex system may take hours and hours to understand and, as there are only two accounts, it would not take long to fully re-perform the reconciliation for each account.

A substantive approach would be better in this case.

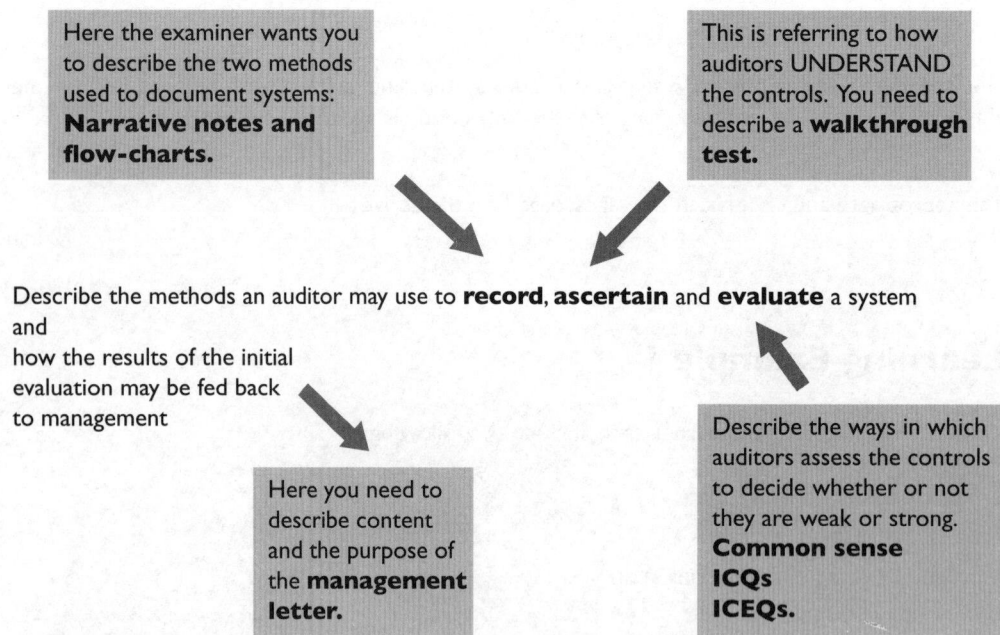

Describe the methods an auditor may use to **record**, **ascertain** and **evaluate** a system and
how the results of the initial evaluation may be fed back to management

### Purchases

The system is strong so a controls approach will be better for the purchases.

Where there is a high volume of transactions, if possible it is better to take a controls approach. Substantive testing here would be time consuming and inefficient.

## Exam Question Debrief: Burden (Wages System)

a) This is a very common way for controls to be examined in F8. The examiner has asked you to **describe the weaknesses** in the wages system and to **recommend improvements**.

- To obtain your mark for describing the weaknesses, you must **state the weakness** and say **why** it is a weakness (i.e. what will be the consequence to the company). Be critical.
- Your recommendation should be **positive and detailed** enough for the company to implement it straight away as a control.

By far the best way to present an answer such as this is in a table (just like the appendix to a real management letter).

Then read through the narrative, noting the weakness as you go. You are aiming for nine weaknesses and nine recommendations: one mark for the description and one for the recommendation.

| Description of weakness | Recommendation |
| --- | --- |
| Two clerks deal with the payroll system. Their duties are not segregated which may lead to duplication or omission of tasks, which is inefficient and could lead to transactions not being recorded. | Clearly segregate duties between the payroll clerks. One clerk should deal with production employees and the other with everyone else. |
| Workers clock themselves in at factory gates so they could be clocking their friends on even if they are not in. This could lead to the company paying for hours that have not been worked. | Have a supervisor oversee the clocking in process so employees can only clock themselves in. |
| Hours worked are recorded on the clock cards. These cards could be lost and the hours not recorded on the system. | The hours should be recorded centrally at the end of each day. There should be a random check back to a sample of clock cards to ensure the hours have been recorded accurately. |
| The hours are entered into the computer once a week and the payroll is produced automatically. There are no checks on the payroll so an error in the input of hours will lead to the wrong wages being paid. | The hours that are input into the computer should be checked back to the clock cards before payroll is authorised. |
| Unused clock cards are kept in a locked cabinet but could easily be stolen and used by employees to record extra hours. This could lead to the wage bill being too high. | The cards should be kept in a locked safe in the personnel department. |
| Only one director signs the cheque for wages, which could lead to collusion between the director and the wage clerk to defraud the company. | The wages cheque should be signed by two directors to minimise the chances of collusion. |
| If wages are paid in cash this increases the risk of theft | Payment of wages should be by electronic bank transfer. |
| The employees do not sign that they have received their wages. The production manager could keep unclaimed cash. | All employees should sign a sheet to say they have received their wages. For any names without a signature the payroll clerk should check that there is a returned pay packet. This process should be observed by a manager. |
| The payroll department are notified of new appointments verbally. Appointments could be faked leading to payment of fictional employees. | Appointments should be formally documented and approved by a director before an employee can be paid. |
| Unclaimed wages are kept in a locked filing cabinet which could be stolen. | Any unpaid cash should be returned to the bank. |

b)  If there are 18 marks available for weaknesses in part a) it may not have escaped your attention that this is a weak system! There are two marks available here for stating that:

- the system is weak;
- controls cannot be relied on and;
- a substantive approach is needed;
- the audit will take longer as substantive procedures are more time consuming.

## Learning Summary

- Watch the video clip 'internal controls'.
- Attempt the two exam standard questions 'Methods' and 'Burden'.

# 6

# Audit
# Sampling

# Context

Auditors do not test every single transaction during the audit of the Financial Statements. Firstly, it would be impractical (and almost impossible!) and secondly, their responsibility is to find **material misstatement**, not all misstatements. So instead of testing each transaction in an account balance, auditors will choose a **sample.**

# Exam Hints

Audit sampling has yet to be examined in the new **F8** exam, however, it could easily be tested as part of a knowledge question or as part of the longer scenario question alongside audit procedures.

# Key Learning Points

- Sampling involves the application of audit procedures to less than 100% of items in an account balance or population such that all items have a chance of selection.
- There are two main types of sampling: statistical and non-statistical.
- Random sampling ensures all items in a population have an equal chance of being selected. A computer programme or random number generator is used to select items from the population.
- Monetary unit sampling is a method of sampling that ensures every monetary unit in a population (e.g. every $ or £) has an equal chance of being chosen.

# Chapter Overview

This chapter covers:

- statistical and non-statistical sampling;
- stratification of account balances;
- acceptable errors;
- extrapolation.

# 6.  Audit Sampling

### Definition

**Audit Sampling** - involves the application of audit procedures to **less than 100% of the items** within an account balance or population such that all items have a chance of selection

A **population** is a set of data about which an auditor wishes to draw a conclusion.

## 6.1  SAMPLING METHODS

There are two main forms of sampling:

1.  statistical sampling;,
2.  non-statistical sampling.

### 6.1.1  STATISTICAL SAMPLING

Statistical sampling refers to any approach that involves the **random** selection of a sample. For F8, there are two methods of statistical sampling:

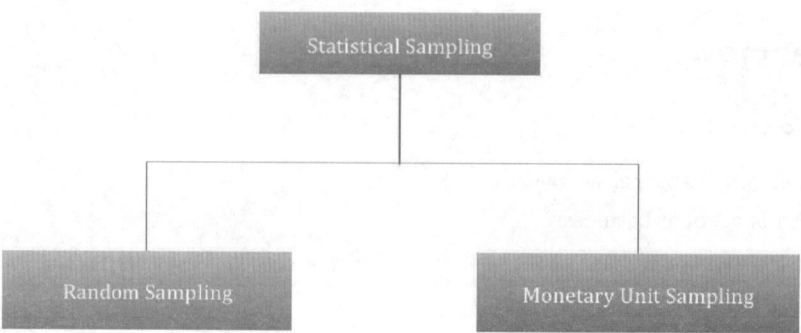

### 6.1.2  RANDOM SAMPLING

Random sampling ensures all items in a population have an equal chance of being selected. A computer programme or random number generator is used to select items from the population.

**Random sampling is used for controls testing.**

## Illustration

During the audit of a client, you are testing the controls operating over the purchases system. One of the control objectives is to ensure that all purchase orders are authorised before being placed and you want to check that this control is working.

Well over 1000 purchase orders have been placed during the year and it would be impractical to test them all so you select a sample of 50 to test. You would use **random** sampling to choose the 50 purchase orders.

We are not concerned about the monetary value of the purchase orders. It is irrelevant as to whether the purchase order is for $10 or $1m. Either the control works or it doesn't. Every purchase order must have a chance of being tested and this is only achieved via random sampling.

### 6.1.3   *MONETARY UNIT SAMPLING*

Monetary unit sampling is a method of sampling that ensures every monetary unit in a population (e.g. every $ or £) has an equal chance of being chosen.

**Monetary unit sampling is used for substantive testing.**

Substantive tests are concerned with checking the numbers in the Financial Statements and, as such, they are concerned with monetary value. It follows then that sampling for substantive tests should also focus on monetary value.

## Illustration

Your client has provided the receivables ledger below. You are to use monetary unit sampling to choose a sample of debtors to circularize.

| Debtor | Balance $'000 |
|--------|---------------|
| A | 9 |
| B | 2 |
| C | 4 |
| D | 3 |
| E | 7 |
| F | 2 |
| G | 2 |
| H | 9 |
| I | 2 |
| J | 22 |
| K | 2 |
| L | 3 |
| M | 6 |
| N | 12 |

In order to perform monetary unit sampling, the auditor must do three things:

1. Progress down the ledger and work out the cumulative balance of receivables (column C overleaf).

2. Set a sampling interval (for example every $10,000).

3. The invoice that includes every 10,000th dollar is chosen for selection (i.e. the invoice containing the $10,000th, $20,000th, $30,000th …..is chosen).

| Debtor | Balance $'000 | Cumulative Balance $'000 | Chosen for sampling |
|--------|---------------|--------------------------|---------------------|
| A | 9 | 9 | |
| B | 2 | 11 | Yes (the first $10k falls between 9K and 11K) |
| C | 4 | 15 | |
| D | 3 | 18 | |
| E | 7 | 25 | Yes (The second $10k falls between 18 and 25) |
| F | 2 | 27 | |
| G | 2 | 29 | |
| H | 9 | 38 | Yes ($30k falls between 29k and 38k) |
| I | 2 | 40 | Yes ($40k falls here) |
| J | 22 | 62 | Yes ($50k and $60k fall between $40k and $62k) |
| K | 2 | 64 | |
| L | 3 | 67 | |
| M | 6 | 73 | Yes ($70k falls between $63k and $70k) |
| N | 12 | 85 | Yes ($80k falls between $73k and $85k) |

The debtors B, E, H, I, J M and I are chosen for sampling.

### 6.1.4   THE SAMPLING INTERVAL

The greater the risk, the **more** we want to test therefore a bigger population is required. To achieve this, the sampling interval should be reduced.

### 6.1.5   NON STATISTICAL SAMPLING

Non-statistical sampling is an approach to sampling where the auditors do not choose items randomly. There is some **judgement** involved for example:

* haphazard selection of items;
* checking a block or sequence of transactions.

### 6.2   OTHER SAMPLING ISSUES

* Stratification.
* Acceptable error rate.
* Extrapolation.

### 6.2.1   STRATIFICATION

Stratification of populations may often be necessary when choosing an appropriate sample.

**Definition**

**Stratification** - the process of dividing a population of items into sub populations, each of which becomes a separate group of sampling items.

London
School of Business
& Finance

shaping success in business and finance

## Illustration

Your client is a large supermarket and you are auditing the figure for wage costs. This figure includes **all** employee wages from shelf stackers all the way up to directors.

You know that directors' salaries are material by nature so you will need to audit the wages of every single director.

If you choose a sample based upon the entire wages population, the chances are your sample will not contain every director. On the other hand, are you going to audit the entire wages population so that you capture all of the directors? No, this would be impractical and unnecessary.

What you would do is to stratify (i.e. break down) the total wages population into two groups:

1. **The directors**, where you would test 100%.
2. **The remaining employees** where you would choose a random sample.

### 6.2.2    *ACCEPTABLE ERROR RATE (TOLERABLE ERROR RATE)*

In a test of control, the acceptable error is the maximum number of times that the control can fail before the auditor concludes that the control is weak and cannot be relied upon.

Often the acceptable error for controls testing is zero. However, if the auditor knows the client systems well and has confidence in them, they may sometimes accept up to two failures in a control and still deem the control to be strong.

In a substantive test, the acceptable error is the maximum monetary error that the auditor is willing to accept in an account balance or class of transactions.

### 6.2.3    *EXTRAPOLATION*

Extrapolation takes the result of a sample and projects that result over the whole population.

Imagine total sales are $10m. You select a sample of $1m (10% of the population) to test. If errors of $37k are found in the sample, it could be inferred by extrapolation that there are errors of $370k in the total population.

**Extrapolation can only be applied to statistical sampling.**

### 6.3    SAMPLING RISK AND NON-SAMPLING RISK

If auditors test a *sample* in order to form an opinion about a *whole population*, then the sample **must be representative.**

**Sampling risk** is the risk that auditor's sample is not representative. Testing a greater number of items, or choosing a more appropriate sampling technique can reduce the risk.

**Non-sampling risk** describes the other factors that can affect the auditor's opinion such as human error and inexperience.

# Exam Question: Audit Sampling

It is important to recognise that audit sampling may be constructed on a non-statistical basis. If the auditor uses statistical sampling, probability theory will be used to ensure each item or $ in value of the population has the same chance of selection.

Non-statistical sampling is more subjective than statistical sampling, typically using haphazard selection methods and placing no reliance on probability theory. However, in certain circumstances statistical-sampling techniques may be difficult to use. The auditor will review the circumstances of each audit before deciding whether to use statistical or non-statistical sampling.

### Required

a)  List three situations where the auditor would be unlikely to use audit-sampling techniques.

3 marks

b)  Explain what you understand by the following terms:

    a.   random sampling;

    b.   monetary unit sampling.

4 marks

c)  Describe the factors which the auditor should consider when determining the size of a sample.

5 marks

d)  Describe to what extent statistical sampling enhances the quality of audit evidence.

4 marks

e)  Explain how judgement is used in statistical and non-statistical sampling.

4 marks

**20 marks**

# Exam Question Debrief: Audit Sampling

a)  Auditors are unlikely to use sampling where:

    i.   They need to test the entire population e.g. directors pay which is material by nature.

    ii.  Risk is high – they may want to test the entire population or focus on known risks e.g. very old debtors.

    iii. The population is small.

b)  **Random Sampling**

This is a technique that ensures that each item in a population has an equal chance of being selected.

Random sampling is used in controls testing as neither controls nor random sampling are interested in monetary value.

### Monetary Unit Sampling

Monetary unit sampling is a method of sampling whereby every $ in a population has an equal chance of being selected.

Monetary unit sampling is used in substantive testing as both are focused on monetary value.

c)  Factors which determine the size of a sample:

    i.   Type of test – controls or substantive.

    ii.  Risk – the bigger the risk, the bigger the sample size.

    iii. Population size (the bigger the population, the bigger the sample).

    iv. Stratification – breaking down a population into its component parts reduces the sample size needed for each part.

    v.  Results – the results of the first few tests may indicate that more testing is needed and the sample size may need to be increased.

d)  How statistic sampling enhances the quality of audit evidence:

    i.   Using statistical sampling is in accordance with the ISAs so therefore can be seen as best practice.

        If the auditor's judgement is called into question (e.g. in a court case, it is easier to defend the use of statistical sampling than other types of sampling).

    ii.  Extrapolation is the process whereby the results of a sample are extrapolated across a whole population. Extrapolation reduced the amount of testing that needs to be done but can only be used with statistical sampling.

e)  **Judgement in Statistical Sampling**

The **selection of items** does not involve any judgement and is completely random.

Judgement does come into statistical sampling, however, because the auditor determines the acceptable error rate, the sample interval and the risk associated with a certain population.

### Judgement in Non-Statistical Sampling

Non-statistical sampling is a non-random method of sampling and as a result will involve some judgement. The auditor may haphazardly choose items in a population for testing but at the same time consciously focus on the riskier items e.g. the older debtors or the higher value items.

# Learning Summary

- Watch the video clip 'audit sampling'.
- Attempt the exam question 'audit sampling'.

# 7

## Internal
## Controls

# Context

In chapter 5 we were introduced to the concept of internal controls and the control environment. We now understand that if auditors can rely on the internal controls they can reduce the amount of substantive testing they need to do. In this chapter we look in detail at the controls operating within individual transaction cycles and how the auditors go about testing these controls. In particular we shall look at:

- the sales system;
- the purchases system;
- the payroll system;
- controls over stock;
- controls over bank and cash.

We also look at the concept of corporate governance and how the internal audit relates to this.

# Exam Hints

Internal controls have been examined in every recent sitting of the F8 examination so ignore this topic at your peril!

In December 2007 students were asked in two separate questions to identify weaknesses in a system for counting stock and petty cash and to recommend control improvements.

In June 2008 students were asked to describe six control tests that auditors would carry out on a sales and despatch system.

In December 2008 students were asked to identify weaknesses and recommend controls for a payroll system.

# Key Learning Points

- The objective of a control is to mitigate a particular risk within a system.
- The control procedure is the **activity** that is carried out to achieve the objective such as a bank reconciliation or an authorisation.
- Tests of controls are performed to evaluate the effectiveness of internal control systems and to ensure that the controls have been operating throughout the period.

# Chapter Overview

This chapter:

- explains the terms control objectives, control procedures and control tests;
- describes in detail individual transaction systems (e.g. sales and purchases) and for each:
  - o details the controls we would expect to see in the system;
  - o describes how the auditor would test these controls;
- discusses corporate governance and internal audit.

# 7. Internal Controls

## 7.1 CONTROL OBJECTIVES, PROCEDURES AND TESTS

In this chapter we shall be looking in detail at controls over several areas of the business. We shall be identifying what controls exist and, most importantly, how auditors test the controls in order to determine whether or not to place reliance on them.

Before we can do this however, we need to understand the terms:

- Control objective;
- Control procedure;
- Control test.

## 7.2 CONTROL OBJECTIVE

The objective of a control is to mitigate a particular risk within a system.

So for example:

| Risk | Control Objective |
|---|---|
| One of the risks in the sales system is that we sell to customers who will not pay. | It follows that the objective is **'to ensure that we only sell to credit-worthy customers'**. |
| A risk in the purchases system is that employees buy goods for their own personal use. | The control objective is **'to ensure that all purchases are for legitimate business use only'**. |

## 7.3 CONTROL PROCEDURES

The control procedure is the **activity** that is carried out to achieve the objective. Using the above examples:

| Risk | Control Objective | Control Procedure |
|---|---|---|
| One of the risks in the sales system is that we sell to customers who will not pay. | It follows that the objective is **'to ensure that we only sell to credit-worthy customers'**. | Credit checks are carried out on all new customers before orders are accepted. |
| A risk in the purchases system is that employees buy goods for their own personal use. | The control objective is **'to ensure that all purchases are for legitimate business use only'**. | All purchase orders must be authorised by a manager before being placed. |

## 7.4 CONTROL TESTS

Tests of these controls are performed to:

- evaluate the effectiveness of the internal control systems; and
- to ensure that the controls have been operating throughout the period.

| Risk | Control Objective | Control Procedure | Control Test |
|------|-------------------|-------------------|--------------|
| One of the risks in the sales system is that we sell to customers who will not pay. | It follows that the objective is **'to ensure that we only sell to credit-worthy customers'**. | Credit checks are carried out on all new customers before orders are accepted. | Auditors inspect the credit references for a sample of new customers in the year. |
| A risk in the purchases system is that employees buy goods for their own personal use. | The control objective is **'to ensure that all purchases are for legitimate business use only'**. | All purchase orders must be authorised by a manager before being placed. | Auditors inspect a sample of purchase orders for evidence of authorisation e.g. a signature. |

Tests of control include:

* inspection;
* enquiries;
* re-performance of control procedures;
* observation of control procedures.

## 7.5 THE SALES SYSTEM

In order to understand the detailed controls operating in the sales system, it is important to understand how a typical sales system works. A simple generic version of the sales system is shown on the next page:

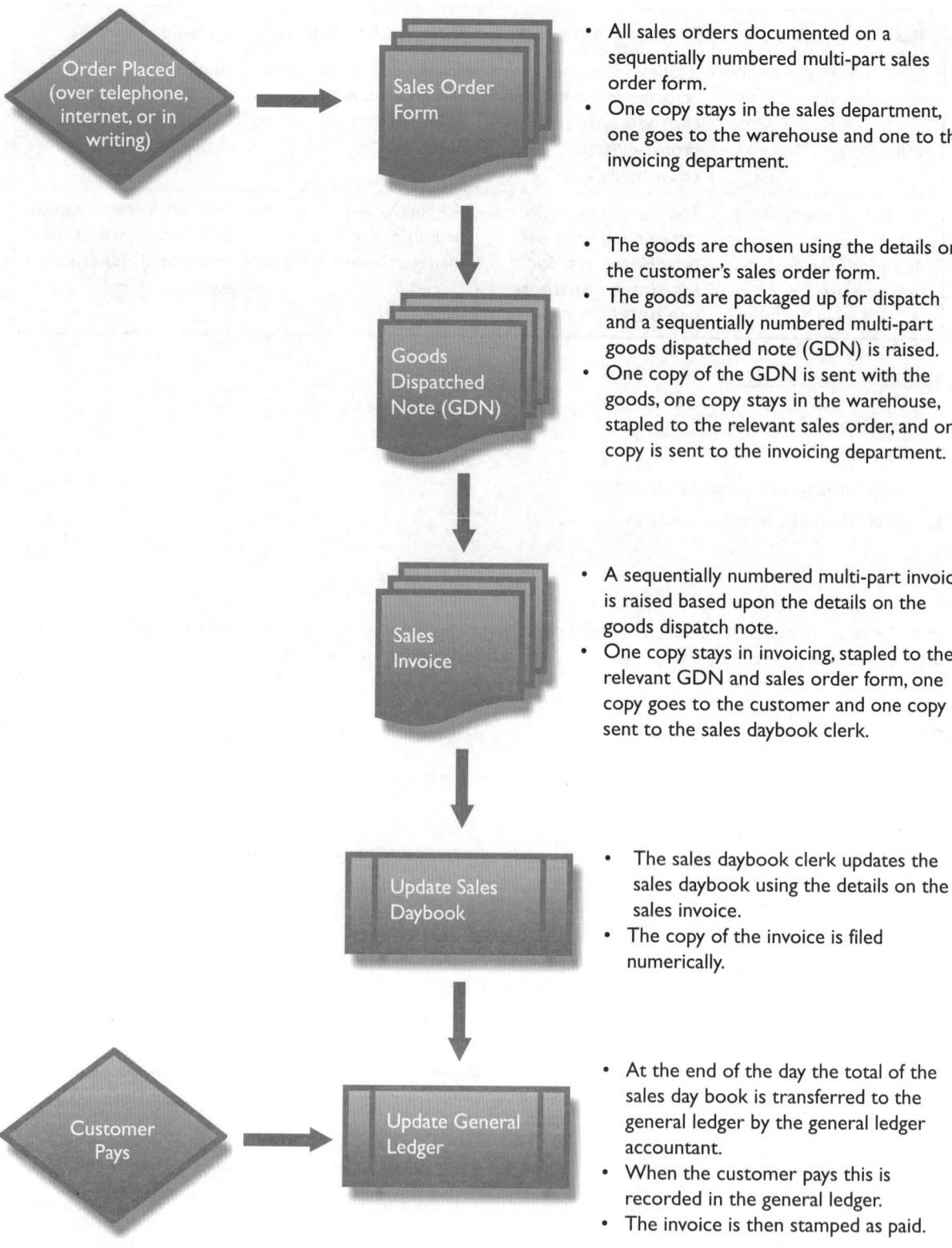

**Order Placed (over telephone, internet, or in writing)** → **Sales Order Form**

- All sales orders documented on a sequentially numbered multi-part sales order form.
- One copy stays in the sales department, one goes to the warehouse and one to the invoicing department.

**Goods Dispatched Note (GDN)**

- The goods are chosen using the details on the customer's sales order form.
- The goods are packaged up for dispatch and a sequentially numbered multi-part goods dispatched note (GDN) is raised.
- One copy of the GDN is sent with the goods, one copy stays in the warehouse, stapled to the relevant sales order, and one copy is sent to the invoicing department.

**Sales Invoice**

- A sequentially numbered multi-part invoice is raised based upon the details on the goods dispatch note.
- One copy stays in invoicing, stapled to the relevant GDN and sales order form, one copy goes to the customer and one copy is sent to the sales daybook clerk.

**Update Sales Daybook**

- The sales daybook clerk updates the sales daybook using the details on the sales invoice.
- The copy of the invoice is filed numerically.

**Customer Pays** → **Update General Ledger**

- At the end of the day the total of the sales day book is transferred to the general ledger by the general ledger accountant.
- When the customer pays this is recorded in the general ledger.
- The invoice is then stamped as paid.

## 7.6 THE SALES CYCLE: CONTROL OBJECTIVES AND PROCEDURES

Now we have seen how the sales system operates, we can start to think about the things that could go wrong at each stage (the risks) and suggest detailed controls to mitigate these risks.

To devise a control objective we simply need to think about what could go wrong. The control objective is to ensure that doesn't happen and the control is the physical activity we need to carry out in order to ensure that it doesn't!

| Stage | Control Objective | Control |
|---|---|---|
| Order placed. | • To ensure that the order details are correct. | • Confirm order back to customer. |
| | • To ensure customer is credit-worthy. | • All new customers must be subject to credit check with recognised agency and approved by sales manager before first order is accepted.<br>• Perform regular credit checks on existing customers. |
| | • To ensure that customers are not over their credit limit when they place an order. | • Credit limits checked before order is accepted.<br>• Programme system to reject a sales order that would breach the customer's credit limit. |
| | • To ensure the order can be fulfilled. | • Check stock records before accepting order and sign sales order form as evidence this has been done. |
| Goods despatched to customer. | • To ensure that all sales orders are sent to the warehouse. | • All sales orders should be sequentially numbered. The warehouse copy should be filed numerically and a regular sequence check carried out to identify missing numbers that have not arrived from the sales ordering department. |
| | • To ensure that the right goods are despatched. | • Choose goods using the copy of the sales order form.<br>• When GDN is raised, match the details to the sales order, sign GDN copy to say this has been done and staple GDN copy and sales order together.<br>• Customer should sign a detachable part of their copy of the GDN and return to seller to say that correct goods have been received. |
| | • To ensure only good quality goods are despatched to customers. | • Goods should be checked for quality before despatch and the GDN signed to say this has been done. |
| | • To ensure goods arrive at customer premises. | • Use reputable delivery firm. |
| Invoice raised. | • To ensure invoiced raised for every despatch. | • Use sequentially numbered GDNs. The copy that is sent to invoicing should be filed numerically and a regular sequence check carried out to identify any missing copies.<br>• All GDNs received by invoicing should be stapled to the relevant invoice once it is raised and the copy of the relevant sales order. A regular check should be carried out for GDNs that do not have invoice attached. |

| Stage | Control Objective | Control |
|---|---|---|
| | • To ensure invoice raised for right amount. | • Invoice should be matched to details on the relevant copy of GDN and relevant copy of sales order and signed to say it has been matched.<br>• Computer system programmed to automatically calculate sales tax on relevant items. |
| Sale is recorded in the accounts. | • To ensure that all sales are recorded in sales day book. | • Use sequentially numbered invoices. The sales daybook clerk should file the copy of the invoice numerically and regularly check for missing invoices. |
| | • To ensure that all sales are recorded at the correct amount. | • All entries in the sales daybook should be checked back to the relevant invoice. A spot check should be carried out by a manager. |
| | • To ensure that all sales are recorded in the general ledger. | • Manager should total invoices at end of every day and check total agrees to total in sales day book.<br>• Perform a debtor's ledger control account reconciliation. |
| | • To ensure sale is recorded against the right debtor in the ledger | • Send customer statements. |
| Cash received. | • To ensure that the customer has paid the correct amount. | • Agree the payment back to the original invoice.<br>• Review the debtor's ledger for credit balances (customer overpaid). |
| | • To ensure that the customer does pay. | • Produce and review aged debtors listing and chase older debts, threatening with legal action if debt remains unpaid. |
| Cash is recorded. | • To ensure that all cash receipts are recorded. | • Send customer statements (customers will tell you if there is a debt that they have actually paid.) |
| | • To ensure that cash is recorded at the correct amount. | • Perform a bank reconciliation which is reviewed by a manager. |
| | • To ensure cash payment is recorded in the correct debtor account. | • Regular spot check of remittance advice to ledger.<br>• Send customer statements (customers will tell you if there is a debt that they have actually paid). |

# Learning Example 1

Describe 10 control tests that the auditors would carry out on the sales system above

London
School of Business
& Finance

shaping success in business and finance

## 7.7 THE PURCHASES SYSTEM

A simple generic version of the purchases system is shown below:

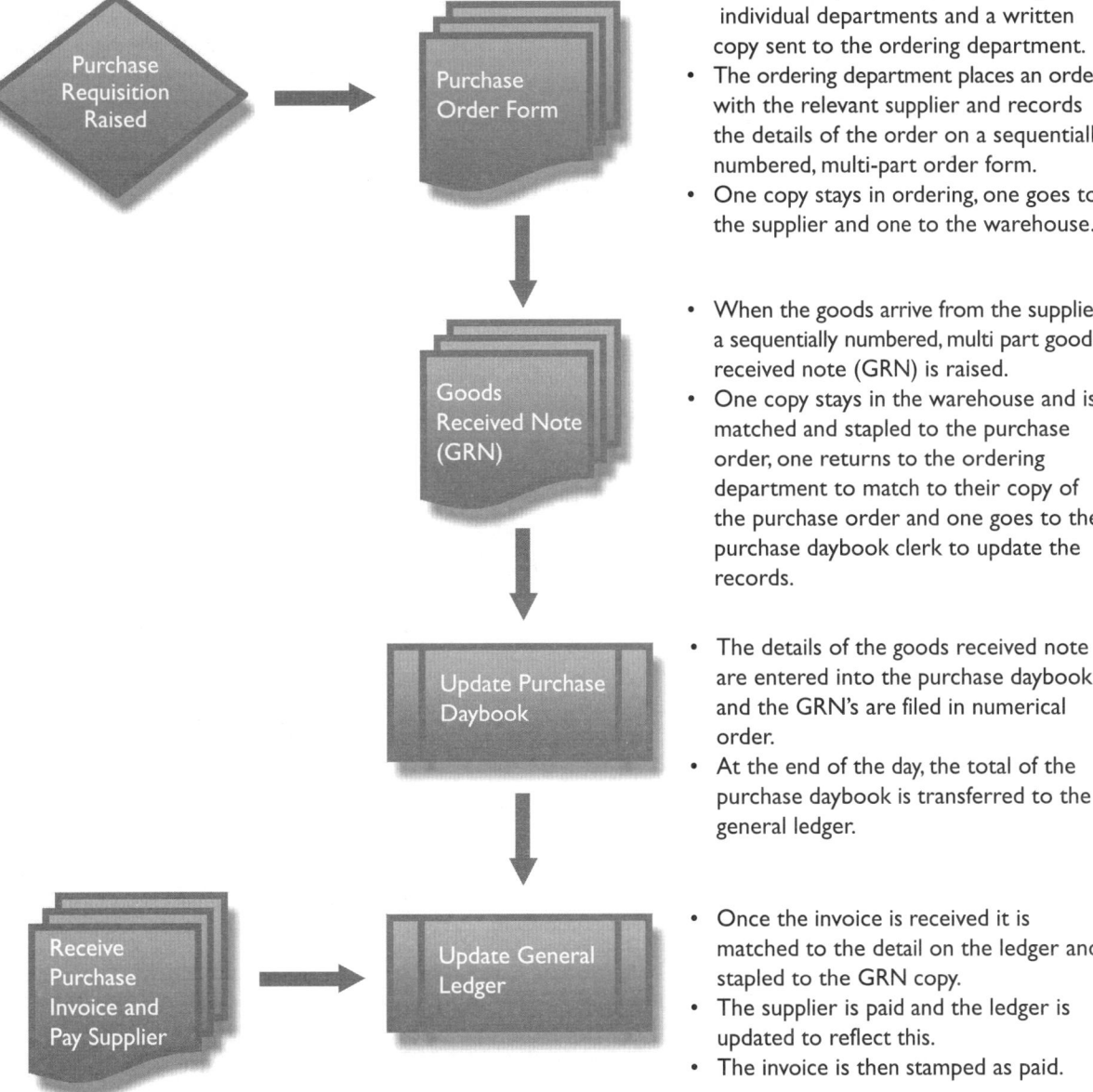

- Purchase requisitions are raised by the individual departments and a written copy sent to the ordering department.
- The ordering department places an order with the relevant supplier and records the details of the order on a sequentially numbered, multi-part order form.
- One copy stays in ordering, one goes to the supplier and one to the warehouse.

- When the goods arrive from the supplier, a sequentially numbered, multi part goods. received note (GRN) is raised.
- One copy stays in the warehouse and is matched and stapled to the purchase order, one returns to the ordering department to match to their copy of the purchase order and one goes to the purchase daybook clerk to update the records.

- The details of the goods received note are entered into the purchase daybook and the GRN's are filed in numerical order.
- At the end of the day, the total of the purchase daybook is transferred to the general ledger.

- Once the invoice is received it is matched to the detail on the ledger and stapled to the GRN copy.
- The supplier is paid and the ledger is updated to reflect this.
- The invoice is then stamped as paid.

| Stage | Control Objective | Control |
|-------|-------------------|---------|
| Requisition raised | • To ensure that requisition is for valid business need. | • All requisitions authorised by department manager and signed as evidence of authorisation. |
| | • To ensure all purchases are cost effective. | • Have central ordering department with approved list of suppliers. |
| | • To ensure items actually needed. | • Department manager checks stock levels before authorising requisition and signs requisition to confirm the check. |

| Stage | Control Objective | Control |
|---|---|---|
| Order is placed. | • To ensure order is raised for each authorised requisition. | • Have sequentially numbered requisition pads, copies filed numerically with copy of order stapled to it. Periodically checked that all requisitions are there and all are matched to a purchase order. |
| | • To ensure orders are accurately recorded by supplier. | • Ask them to confirm order with you. |
| | • To ensure all items are correctly costed. | • Check quoted price to approved supplier list. |
| Goods received. | • To ensure goods received for each order. | • Copy of purchase order sent to warehouse, sequentially numbered, filed, stapled and matched to GRN. Regular checks that all are there.<br>• Have one delivery area to minimise chances of goods being mislaid. |
| | • To ensure that the goods received are of right quality and quantity. | • Raise GRN and grid stamp and sign once goods have been checked to purchase order details. |
| Purchase recorded. | • To ensure purchase recorded for all goods received. | • Copy of GRN sent to purchase daybook clerk sequentially numbered. Regular checks that all are there.<br>• All entries in the purchase daybook should be checked back to the relevant GRN. A spot check should be carried out by a manager.<br>• Manager should total GRNs at end of every day and check total agrees to total in sales day book. |
| | • To ensure total of purchase day book recorded accurately in general ledger. | • Perform a supplier's ledger control account reconciliation. Reviewed by manager. |
| | • To ensure purchase recorded against the correct supplier. | • Reconcile supplier statements to the detail in the general ledger.<br>• Perform a debtor's ledger control account reconciliation. |
| Invoice received. | • To ensure that invoices are received for all goods received. | • Relevant invoice stapled to all GRNs in purchase daybook clerk's file.<br>• Regular checks to ensure all GRNs have matching invoice. |
| | • To ensure we don't get invoices for things we have not received. | • Match all invoices to a GRN. Follow up on any invoices received where there is no matching GRN. |
| Cash paid. | • To ensure all invoices paid. | • Stamp all invoices when paid and check all invoices stamped. |
| | • To ensure invoices only paid once. | • Stamp all invoices when paid and keep paid invoices separate from unpaid ones. |
| | • To ensure paid correct amount. | • Cheque signatory to match details of cheque to the relevant invoice. |

| Stage | Control Objective | Control |
|---|---|---|
| Cash recorded. | • To ensure all payments are recorded in the cash book. | • Perform a bank reconciliation. |
| | • To ensure payments are recorded against the correct supplier account. | • Perform a supplier statement reconciliation. |

## 7.8  TESTS OF CONTROL FOR PURCHASES

Tests of controls over purchases include:

- inspect a sample of requisition forms for evidence of authorisation;
- inspect a sample of requisition forms for evidence of signature showing stock records were checked;
- inspect a sample of GRNs for signature showing someone checked it back to the purchase order form;
- observe goods received process for evidence of quality and quantity check;
- inspect a sample of purchase invoices for evidence they have been checked back to the GRN and purchase order;
- obtain the GRN file from the purchase daybook clerk and review the GRNs to ensure they are all there and in sequence;
- obtain and re-perform the supplier's control account reconciliation;
- obtain the file of paid invoices and inspect to make sure all invoices stamped as being paid.

# Learning Example 2

You are the senior in charge of the audit of Dean Ltd. To assist you in your audit planning one of the audit team had provided the following description of the purchasing system. No other controls exist apart from those described.

**Identify six weaknesses and briefly explain their audit significance.**

"The company has no buying department so employees place orders in their own area of responsibility. A three part order form is used; original, copy two is sent to the goods inwards department and copy three is sent to the supplier."

"Goods are received, but not checked, by the goods inwards clerk. Once received, the advice note and purchase order for those goods are sent to the purchase ledger clerk."

"When the supplier's invoice is received the purchase ledger clerk checks the calculations on it, initials it and staples the advice note and purchase order to it. She enters the invoice onto the purchase ledger."

"The invoice is then sent to the manager responsible for the employee who ordered the goods. The manager codes the invoice and returns it to the purchase ledger clerk. Purchase invoices are coded, entered on an analysis sheet and posted to the nominal ledger monthly by journal entry."

"The cashier pays suppliers monthly on instructions from the purchase ledger clerk. The purchase ledger control account is reconciled monthly by the purchase ledger clerk who also reconciles suppliers statements."

## 7.9    THE PAYROLL SYSTEM

Payroll is essentially a mechanical exercise with standard calculations being done for each employee. It is typically completed using computer software. Assuming the software is reliable, the main problems with payroll are likely to occur with the **input of information** into the system.

The following is a basic representation of a generic payroll system:

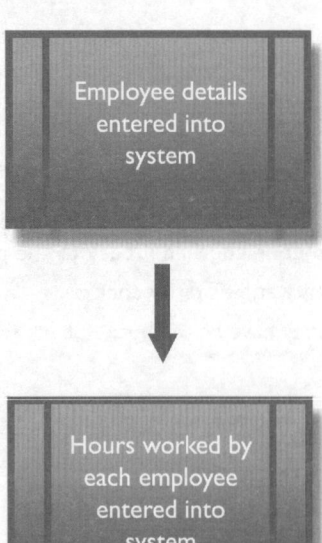

- Employee names, addresses, annual salaries or hourly rates, tax and banking details will be needed every time payroll is run. These details are kept permanently on the system. This is known as standing data.
- Details of new employees are added and details of leavers are removed.

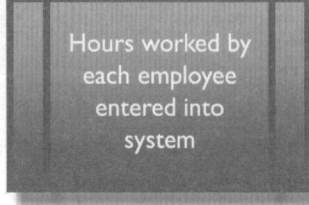

- For hourly employees, the details of the hours worked are recorded on clock cards or time. sheets and these details are input into the system
- The pay rate for salaried employees is worked out by reference to their contract.

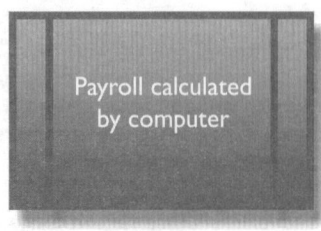

- The wages of each employee along with the relevant PAYE and national insurance. contributions are calculated by the system
- The PAYE and National insurance liabilities are automatically recorded in the ledgers.

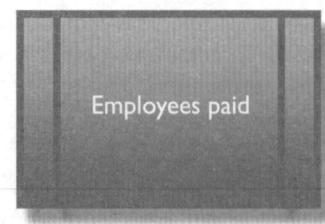

- Using the figures calculated by the system the employees are paid by bank transfer (preferable), cheque or cash.

| Stage | Control Objective | Control |
|-------|-------------------|---------|
| Details of employees are added to the system. | • To ensure only legitimate new employees are added to the system. | • For every new employee there must be a new joiner's form filled in and signed by the Human Resources Director. This form contains all their details and is filed with a copy of their contract and a photograph in an employee file.<br><br>• The HR director should approve all new additions to the system by signing the new joiners form before the payroll manager enters them onto the system.<br><br>• A list of joiners and leavers entered onto the system should be printed every week and reviewed by the HR director.<br><br>• The HR manager should regularly carry out spot checks by choosing names from the system and ensuring there is a corresponding employee file and the details match. |
| | • To ensure all leavers are taken off the system. | • A leavers form should be filled out and the details of this employee removed from the system by the payroll manager. This should be checked by the HR director.<br><br>• Leavers' files should be archived away from current employee files.<br><br>• Regularly reconcile the number of people on the payroll to the number of current employee files in the HR department. |
| | • To ensure standing data is not corrupted or changed fraudulently. | • A hierarchy of passwords should protect the payroll system. Clerks should have access to input hours worked only, managers and directors should have access to change standing data.<br><br>• Any request to change standing data must be submitted in writing to the HR director who must approve this in writing before the manager makes the changes on the system.<br><br>• A print-out of changes to standing data should be obtained once a week. The HR director should match the changes to the written approval.<br><br>• Regular spot checks of standing data to other evidence e.g. employee contract. |

| Stage | Control Objective | Control |
|-------|-------------------|---------|
| Hours are entered. | • To ensure that employees are only paid for hours worked. | • Clocking in and out should be supervised.<br>• Clock card machine to be in an open location, possibly with CCTV, to discourage staff from clocking in their friends.<br>• Clock cards should be kept locked in a safe when not in use.<br>• Only clock cards and time sheets authorised by department managers may be entered onto the system.<br>• Overtime to be authorised by department managers in advance. |
| Salaries are calculated by the system. | • To ensure that the correct salaries are calculated. | • System produces a net pay list which is reviewed by department managers.<br>• System to produce exception reports (e.g. any employee working over 70 hours a week) which are reviewed to identify potential errors. |
| Employees are paid | • To ensure employees receive payment. | • Staff to be paid by bank transfer if possible. |
| | • To ensure any cash kept on premises is not stolen. | • If staff paid in cash, the cash to be stored in a safe.<br>• Where staff paid in cash, staff required to sign to confirm receipt.<br>• Segregate duties in the payroll department: one person inputs the hours, another counts out cash, another distributes the cash to employees. |

## 7.10 TESTS OF CONTROL FOR PAYROLL

Tests of controls over payroll include:

- select a sample of new joiner forms and inspect for evidence they have been signed by the HR director;
- obtain the weekly print out of joiners and leavers and inspect for evidence that the HR director has authorised the changes to the system;
- observe the clocking in and clocking out process;
- Inspect clock cards and timesheets for evidence of manager approval;
- obtain the exception reports produced by the system and inspect for evidence that exceptions have been followed up and resolved;
- carry out some test data on the system (see chapter 13);
- obtain the list of employees paid in cash and inspect for their signature that wages have been received.

## 7.11 INVENTORY

The basic control objectives over inventory are to ensure:

- that inventory is not stolen;
- that inventory is not damaged;
- that inventory records are accurate.

London School of Business & Finance
shaping success in business and finance

Examples of controls that achieve these objectives include:

- keeping valuable inventory items in secure warehouses with CCTV;
- security guard patrols;
- where necessary, ensure inventory kept at correct temperature;
- train staff in how to handle delicate inventory;
- regular inventory counts (stock-takes) and comparison of the results to inventory records.

## 7.12 INVENTORY COUNTS

The counting of inventory can be done at different times throughout the year.

### Annual year end inventory count

This is perhaps the most obvious. Every single item is counted as close to the accounting year end as possible. The benefit of the annual inventory count is that its can be used by auditors as evidence over the inventory balance in the year end Financial Statements.

### Continuous Inventory Counting

Continuous inventory counting, as the name suggests, is where a company counts parts of its inventories every few weeks. The aim being that over the course of the year all items are checked. This is less disruptive to the business than a full count.

### Full count near the year end

This is sometimes necessary where the year end date is not appropriate (e.g. the company is too busy at the year end). The figures counted are rolled forward/back by adding or subtracting purchases and sales between the count and the year end date.

## 7.13 NON-CURRENT ASSETS

Purchases of non-current assets are controlled in the same way as regular purchases. The only main differences are:

- Capital expenditure is likely to have been budgeted for at the start of the year, as it is a significant expense to the company. A powerful control is to compare the actual spend to budgeted spend. Any major differences may signify errors in recording the actual figures or weaknesses in the budgeting process.
- Non-current assets will need to be checked more thoroughly for quality on arrival.
- Due to the significant cost to the company of purchasing non-current assets, authorisation is essential before any orders are placed.

## 7.14 BANK AND CASH

The basic control objectives over bank and cash are to ensure that:

- money is not stolen;
- money received is paid into company bank accounts quickly;
- any payments made are for genuine business purposes and not, for example, payments to fictitious employees or suppliers set up for fraudulent reasons.

Examples of controls that achieve these objectives include:

- any cash kept on company premises is kept in a locked safe;
- where there are tills, these are:
  - o locked when no staff are present;
  - o have the pries of products pre-programmed;
  - o only accessible to authorised staff with a key or swipe card;
  - o reconciled daily (till record v actual cash takings);
- cash taken to bank using security form;
- list of approved signatures for each bank account;
- regular bank reconciliations;
- cheque payments above a certain amount need two signatories.

## 7.15 CORPORATE GOVERNANCE

Corporate governance is the system by which companies are directed and controlled.

## 7.16 THE NEED FOR STRONG CORPORATE GOVERNANCE

In the case of many companies, the people controlling the company (the directors) are separate from those who own it (the shareholders).

In the largest organisations, some owners may have such small **individual stakes** that:

- they only have the chance to find out about how the company is being run at the AGM;
- they may not be prepared to challenge the directors;
- they may not have the power to challenge the directors.

The largest owners of companies are often **institutional shareholders** (e.g. pension funds). These institutional shareholders are usually investing money on behalf others (not their own money) so often, they do not take an active interest in how the company is being run.

In addition globalization has resulted in many of the world's largest companies and organisations becoming even larger than they were in the past.

High profile **corporate failures** (e.g. Enron and WorldCom), the apparent increase in **corporate fraud** (e.g. Maxwell and the Mirror Group) and unethical business practices have lead to a lack of trust in directors.

With these issues in mind, **corporate governance rules and guidelines** have been developed. These rules and guidelines aim to ensure directors manage companies in the best interest of the owners and other stakeholders.

## 7.17 CORPORATE GOVERNANCE RULES AND GUIDELINES

### 7.17.1 *WHO SET THE RULES?*

- **Global**: The OECD (Organisation for Economic Co-operation and Development) have developed a code.
- **National**: Many countries have developed their own guidelines, sometimes theses are imposed under statute (law) (e.g. Sarbanes-Oxley in the USA) and sometimes as a Code (guidelines for best practice) (e.g. The Combined Code in the UK).
- **Companies**: Many companies have developed their own policies on corporate governance, some of which go further than the rules of the code their own country expects them to follow.
- **Other**: In some countries, something that appears to be "voluntary" can effectively become law (e.g. in UK all listed companies are required to either follow the Combined Code, or explain why they have not followed it (Stock Exchange Rules)).

## 7.18   UNDERLYING CONCEPTS BEHIND CORPORATE GOVERNANCE

These are the fundamental principles behind how companies and directors should behave. These are discussed below:

| | |
|---|---|
| **Fairness** | All people affected by a company's decisions (i.e. it's stakeholders) should be treated with equal consideration. |
| **Openness and transparency** | All information should have been made available to stakeholders and in a dear manner. <br><br> This may suggest companies should not just follow **disclosure** rules, but also add voluntary disclosures if it improves transparency. |
| **Independence** | All those in a position of monitoring should be independent of those whom they are monitoring: <br><br> •   Non-executive Directors should be independent of the Executives, and of company operations. <br><br> •   External auditors should be independent of the company, especially its accounting department and processes. <br><br> •   Internal auditors should be as independent as possible. |
| **Probity/ Honesty** | Directors should always be truthful with stakeholders |
| **Responsibility** | Directors should understand and accept their responsibility to shareholders and other stakeholders, act in their best interests and be willing to accept the consequences if they fail in this responsibility. |
| **Accountability** | This links with responsibility. Directors must be willing to be held accountable for their actions. |
| **Reputation** | Directors must protect their own reputation, and that of the company they run, as damage to either is likely to lead to more widespread damage to the company. This raises an interesting debate about whether a director's private life is in fact private, since a bad personal reputation is likely to affect their business reputation and hence that of the company. |
| **Integrity** | This is quite a general term and has a crossover with some of the other terms above. <br><br> Integrity means honesty, fair-dealing, presenting information without any attempt to bias opinion and in a more general sense, doing the right thing. |
| **Judgement** | Directors must ensure they have all the necessary information and understanding in order to be able to make sensible business decisions that improve the prosperity of the company. |

### 7.19 THE MAIN AREAS OF CORPORATE GOVERNANCE

Using the UK Combined Code as an example, the primary areas of Corporate Governance cover:

#### 7.19.1 *DIRECTORS*

Every company should have an effective board of directors which:

- should lead company strategy;
- should include Non-executive Directors (NEDSs) who:
  - o contribute to strategy;
  - o assess performance of Executive Directors;
  - o oversee the integrity of financial information, control systems, and risk management;
  - o decide remuneration of Executive Directors;
  - o appoint, remove, and consider succession planning of Executive Directors;
- should meet regularly, with a formal agenda;
- should detail its membership (including Chairman, CEO, Senior Independent;
- director, Committee members) and work in Annual Report;
- should ensure Chairman and NEDs meet without the Executives, to consider their performance;
- should ensure NEDs meet without Chairman annually, to consider performance of Chairman.

#### 7.19.2. *CHAIRMAN AND CHIEF EXECUTIVE OFFICER*

- should not be the same person;
- chairman leads the Board, and sets agenda for Board meetings;
- chairman is key contact for shareholders;
- chairman is independent on appointment;
- chairman is not the former CEO of the company;
- CEO runs the company.

#### 7.19.3 *BOARD BALANCE*

- no one person, or group, should be able to dominate the Board;
- at least half of the Board, excluding the Chairman, should be independent NEDs;
- there should be an appropriate balance of skills and experience;
- the Annual Report must detail which NEDs are considered independent;
- the Board should appoint a Senior Independent Director, so shareholders have an alternative to talking to the Chairman.

#### 7.19.4 *APPOINTMENTS TO THE BOARD*

- should be done by a nomination Committee, the majority of whom are independent NEDs;
- chaired by Chairman (unless Chairman is being discussed);
- have criteria for selection of new Board members;
- report its work in the Annual Report;
- organise induction and training for all directors.

#### 7.19.5 *ANNUAL PERFORMANCE REVIEW*

- the Board, its committees, and individual directors should have performance appraised at least annually.

#### 7.19.6 *RE-ELECTION OF BOARD MEMBERS*

- should take place at first AGM after appointment to Board, and then at least every three years afterwards;
- appointment of directors should be approved by the shareholders.

### 7.19.7  REMUNERATION OF DIRECTORS

- should be enough to attract, retain and motivate but not excessive;
- significant proportion should be performance related;
- should consider industry pay levels;
- NED remuneration should not be performance related, but should reflect time involvement of the role;
- if a director is removed before the end of contract, provisions should be in place to ensure they are not over-compensated for failure;
- notice periods no longer than one year.

### 7.19.8  REMUNERATION COMMITTEE

- should be made up of at least three independent NEDs as members;
- should set remuneration of all executive directors and the Chairman, and Senior Management;
- remuneration of NEDs is flexible – could be by Board as a whole, by shareholders, or a separate Board Committee;
- shareholders must approve any long-term share options.

### 7.19.9  FINANCIAL REPORTING

- Board should present a balanced assessment of company's position and future prospects.

### 7.19.10  INTERNAL CONTROL

- Board should ensure a sound system of internal controls;
- there should be an annual review of effectiveness of internal controls, and this should be recorded in the Annual Report.

### 7.19.11  AUDIT COMMITTEE AND AUDIT

- there should be an Audit Committee made up at least three independent NEDs;
- at least one member of the committee is to have recent relevant financial experience;
- main role is liaison with the internal and external auditors on all matters.

### 7.19.12  RELATIONS WITH SHAREHOLDERS

- the Directors should enter into regular dialogue with shareholders;
- Chairman to ensure shareholder views communicated to Board.

### 7.19.13  CONSTRUCTIVE USE OF AGM

- the AGM should be used to communicate with investors;
- debate of the issues should be encouraged;
- allow the use of proxy votes for those who are unable to attend.

### 7.19.14  INSTITUTIONAL SHAREHOLDERS

- should themselves ensure dialogue with directors;
- should make considered use of their considerable voting power.

## 7.20 AUDIT COMMITTEES

For F8, the main areas of corporate governance we are interested in are the involvement of external and internal audit and this introduces the concept of audit committees.

The audit committee's role is to be the liaison between the Board of Directors and both sets of auditors. As such, it is likely to:

- shortlist a firm of external auditors for the shareholder vote at the AGM;
- monitor the independence of the external auditors;
- negotiate a fee proposal for the external audit;
- receive the external auditor's report, management letter, and any other communication;
- decide on the resources needed for internal audit;
- decide whether to use in-house internal audit or to outsource the role to a third party;
- recruit the Chief Internal Auditor;
- receive all internal audit reports;
- overall, monitor the financial reporting and internal control systems of a company;

By having auditors liaise with the audit committee rather than with the Board directly, the independence and effectiveness of the audit functions should be improved.

## 7.21 INVOLVEMENT OF EXTERNAL AUDIT IN GOVERNANCE

Corporate Governance rules/guidelines typically state that:

- a company should produce a balanced annual report;
- companies should have a "sound" system of internal controls.

In these two areas, external auditors can play an important role. They form an opinion on the annual Financial Statements, and may be asked to give opinions on other areas of the Annual Report.

In producing a management letter, auditors are assisting management in their duty to have effective internal control systems.

In a wider sense, the external auditors are in a position to advise clients on whether corporate governance rules/guidelines are being followed.

## 7.22 INVOLVEMENT OF INTERNAL AUDIT IN GOVERNANCE

Internal audit is part of an effective risk management and internal control system, a central area of good corporate governance. As such, internal audit does not just assist good governance, it is an integral part of it.

## 7.23 THE ROLE OF INTERNAL AUDIT

Internal audit can be used to carry out a variety of roles within the organisation including:

- monitoring internal control;
- monitoring the company's compliance with laws and regulations such as the corporate governance requirements;
- fraud investigations;
- examining financial information;
- review of the economy and efficiency of the company's operations.;
- reporting to the Board on whether the internal management accounting systems are producing reliable information.

## 7.24 ISSUES WITH INTERNAL AUDIT

### 7.24.1 INDEPENDENCE

Although in many cases, the internal audit department is staffed by people working for the company, they still need to be as independent as they possibly can from the areas they are reviewing.

In particular internal auditors should:

- monitor and review controls, not design and implement them;
- report to the audit committee if possible, not the finance director;
- be free to decide on the nature and scope of their work;
- be free to communicate fully with the external auditors.

### 7.24.2 EXTERNAL AUDIT RELIANCE ON INTERNAL AUDIT WORK

It is likely that the internal auditors will do some work that is useful to the external auditors, who may therefore choose to rely on rather than repeat it.

Examples include:

- testing of the accuracy of management accounts during the year;
- controls testing throughout the year;
- attendance at the inventory count attendance (e.g. if there are many locations, the external and internal auditors could share them out to ensure that some auditors are attending as many as possible).

Before relying on the work of Internal Audit, the external auditors will need to consider:

- their experience;
- their qualifications;
- whether or not they act on the issues raised;
- whether or not their recommendations are taken seriously by the company and implemented;
- the quality of their work – including whether or not their work is properly planned, supervised and documented.

### 7.24.3 OUTSOURCING DECISION

Should company have its own in-house internal audit department, or should it pay outside experts to supply internal audit service as and when it is needed?

### 7.24.4 ADVANTAGES OF OUTSOURCING

- saves paying full time salaries and other associate staff costs;
- get the expertise of the outside specialists;
- should improve the independence of internal audit work;
- get the experience of internal auditors who have recently seen inside other companies.

### 7.24.5 DISADVANTAGES OF OUTSOURCING

- can be expensive if company has a lot of internal audit work to do;
- cost of monitoring people outside the company;
- cost of researching an outside firm, creating a legal agreement, monitoring quality;
- risk of confidentiality breaches;
- cultural difference between outsource partner and company;
- may be slower to respond than internal staff.

# Exam Question: Bingham (Sales System)

Your firm is the external auditor of Bingham Wholesale, and you have been assigned to the audit of the sales system. Bingham Wholesale purchases textile products (e.g. clothes) from manufacturers and sells them to retailers.

An initial review of the sales system has shown that control risk is likely to be low with sufficient staff to achieve a proper division of duties. Thus, the audit manager has decided that the audit approach should be to record, evaluate and perform extensive tests of controls.

If these confirm controls are effective, control risk will be low, so only restricted substantive procedures will be carried out.

The company have a computerised accounting system which records purchases and sales transactions and maintains records of debtors, creditors and stock (both quality and value). Access to the computer for retrieval of information and input of data is through terminals.

**Required**

Describe 10 control tests you would use, on controls you would expect to see in operation over sales, from ordering to final cash collection.

**(20 marks)**

London
School of Business
& Finance

shaping success in business and finance

# Solution to Learning Example 1

Inspect a copy of the external credit check for a sample of new customers in the year to ensure all new customer are being credit checked.

Try to enter a sales transaction into the system that breaches a customer credit limit – it should be rejected.

Observe staff taking sales orders to ensure they confirm details with the customer.

Inspect a file of sales orders sent to the warehouse to ensure they are filed in numerical order.

Observe warehouse staff using copies of sales orders to choose goods to ensure that the correct goods are chosen.

Select a sample of GDNs and inspect to see if they have been matched and stapled to the relevant sales order and signed by the employee carrying out the task.

Select a sample of GDNs in the accounts department and inspect to ensure an invoice is attached.

Select a file of invoices and review the number sequence to ensure they are all there. Investigate missing invoices.

Observe credit control staff chasing up old receivables.

Inspect legal correspondence with customers whose debts have not been paid.

# Solution to Learning Example 2

NB The example asks for the **audit significance** of the weakness. In the second column you should be thinking about how the weakness may lead to material errors in the Financial Statements (not just inconvenience for the company).

| Weakness | Audit Significance |
|---|---|
| Purchase orders are not authorised. | Employees may purchase goods for their own personal use using the company account. As a result, there will be an accounting mismatch between inventories and purchases. |
| No central buying department. | Different departments may duplicate purchases so the company ends up with too much stock, which then becomes obsolete. |
| Purchase order forms are not sequentially numbered. | If purchase orders are misplaced this will not be identified by a sequence check and the auditors will lose their audit trail. |
| Goods not checked for quality on arrival. | May end up accepting poor quality goods, which cannot be resold therefore affecting the evaluation of inventories. |
| No goods received notes are generated. | The details on the invoice may not match the actual goods received and there is no way of checking. The purchases figure may be misstated as a result. |
| There is no purchase daybook and the ledger is updated monthly. | If purchase transactions are not recorded regularly, details may be lost or forgotten. |
| There is a lack of segregation of duties in the purchase ledger department. | The purchase ledger clerk may be able to cover up a fraud that leads to a material misstatement. |

# Exam Question Debrief: Bingham

This is one of the more difficult types of question regarding controls that you may see in the exam. You are given little information about the company and asked to describe 10 control tests for 20 marks. Each test will be worth two marks so needs to be sufficiently detailed.

The way to approach this is to make sure you understand how a typical sales system works. First think about the **controls you would expect** to see and then **how you would test that control**.

Use the mnemonic ODIACO if it helps you to remember the stages of the system

**O**rdering

**D**espatch/Receipt of goods

**I**nvoicing

**A**ccounts

**C**ash

**O**verall controls (e.g. internal audit)

**Ordering**

- To ensure that all new customers are credit checked before being allowed to order, select a sample of new customers and inspect the credit references.

- To ensure that inventory levels are checked before accepting an order, inspect a sample of purchase orders for evidence of a signature confirming that the check has been carried out.

**Despatch**

- To ensure that a GDN is raised for each despatch, select a sample of sales orders and inspect to ensure a GDN is attached.
- To ensure that the quality of goods is checked before despatch observe the process on a number of occasions.

**Invoices**

- To ensure a sales invoice is raised for each despatch, sample a number of GDN's and inspect to ensure an invoice is attached.
- To ensure that the correct sales tax has been calculated, inspect a sample of invoices and recalculate the sales tax.

**Accounts**

- To ensure that the aged debtors analysis is produced and reviewed, inspect the aged debtors listing for each month end and inspect notes of telephone conversations chasing the old debts.
- To ensure that the receivables ledger control account reconciliation is performed every month end, inspect them and re-perform them for each month end.

**Cash**

- Ensure that cheques received in the post are banked daily by agreeing the date in the paying in book to the date on a sample of cheques from the cheques received listing.
- Ensure that a bank reconciliation is carried out at every month end by inspecting the bank reconciliations for the year.

## Learning Summary

- Watch the video clip 'internal controls'.
- Attempt the exam questions 'Bingham'.

8

# Non-Current
# Assets

London
School of Business
& Finance

shaping success in business and finance

# Context

Once the auditors have assessed the client's internal controls, they are then in a position to determine how much substantive testing needs to be carried out. The following six chapters will look at the procedures the auditors use to substantively test the main areas of the Financial Statements, starting with non-current assets. Non-current assets, both tangible and intangible are likely to be a material balance on the balance sheet. The auditor will check whether the assets exist, whether they are valued correctly and whether the correct costs have been capitalised. Auditors will also focus on testing the depreciation charge, which is likely to be a material expense in the income statement.

# Exam Hints

Substantive audit procedures will mainly be examined in the long 30-mark scenario question. Students must be comfortable with generating substantive procedures for the main balances in the Financial Statements.

In December 2008 students were asked to identify four assertions relevant to non-current assets and to describe four procedures to test these assertions.

# Key Learning Points

- The key risk with non-current assets is overstatement therefore auditors must pay particular attention to existence, ownership and valuation.
- Existence tends to be tested by physical verification
- Analytical procedures are useful for testing depreciation. Auditors can recalculate the depreciation charge and also compare the company's depreciation policy to other companies in the same industry

# Chapter Overview

This chapter:

- Recaps the concepts of audit evidence first seen in chapter 4;
- Describes substantive audit procedures for non-current assets.

# 8. Recap

In Chapter 4 we were introduced to the idea of audit evidence. In order for audit evidence to be useful to auditors it needs to have three characteristics:

1. it needs to be **sufficient** (i.e. we need enough of it to reach our conclusion on the balances in the Financial Statements;

2. it must come from a **reliable** source;

3. it must be relevant (i.e. it needs to test one of the financial statement assertions).

## 8.1 THE FINANCIAL STATEMENT ASSERTIONS

The auditors must test the balances in the **Income Statement** for:

- occurrence;
- completeness;
- accuracy;
- cut-off;
- classification;
- presentation and disclosure.

The auditors must test items on the **balance sheet** for:

- existence;
- completeness;
- rights and obligations (ownership);
- valuation;
- presentation and disclosure.

We saw that the simple mnemonic PROVE can be used to help to remember *some* of the assertions:

**P** Presentation and Disclosure.

**R** Records must be **accurate** and **complete**.

**O** Ownership.

**V** Valuation.

**E** Existence.

In order to obtain their evidence, auditors can use a number of techniques. These are best remembered using the mnemonic AEIOU:

**A** Analytical procedures (i.e. making comparisons and following up unexpected relationships).

**E** Enquiry and confirmation (asking questions of management and confirming their answers with other sources of evidence).

**I** Inspection (looking at the detail on invoices, ledgers etc).

**O** Observation (watching employees perform their roles).

**U** Computation (recalculation of the clients' numbers to see if they are correct).

In the next five chapters, we shall draw on these ideas to design substantive procedures to test different balances in the Financial Statements. For the F8 exam you will need to be able to produce audit procedures for:

- tangible non-current assets (PPE);
- inventories;
- trade receivables (and sales);
- trade creditors (and purchases);
- cash.

This chapter will focus on the audit procedures for testing tangible non-current assets.

## 8.2    TANGIBLE NON-CURRENT ASSETS (PPE)

The **total net book value (i.e. cost less accumulated depreciation)** of PPE is presented in the top half of the balance sheet.

In the notes to the Financial Statements, the total balance of these assets is broken down into assets of different categories also showing any additions, disposals and depreciation during the year. The Financial Statements must also disclose the depreciation policies that the company uses.

An example of a PPE disclosure note is shown below:

|  | Freehold Land and Buildings $ | Plant and Machinery $ | Motor Vehicles $ | Total $ |
|---|---|---|---|---|
| **Cost or Valuation** |  |  |  |  |
| At beginning of year | 500,000 | 200,000 | 75,000 | 775,000 |
| Additions | 200,000 | 100,000 | 25,000 | 325,000 |
| Disposals | - | (50,000) | (10,000) | (60,000) |
| **At end of year** | **700,000** | **250,000** | **90,000** | **1,040,000** |
| **Depreciation** |  |  |  |  |
| At beginning of year | 150,000 | 50,000 | 15,000 | 215,000 |
| Charge for year | 25,000 | 10,000 | 5,000 | 40,000 |
| On disposals | - | (5,000) | (2,000) | (7,000) |
| **At end of year** | **175,000** | **55,000** | **18,000** | **248,000** |
| **Net book value at end of year** | **525,000** | **195,000** | **72,000** | **792,000** |

This figure goes to the face of the Balance Sheet.

## 8.3    THE FIXED ASSET REGISTER

A well controlled company will also keep a register of all of their plant, property and equipment. This will contain all relevant information about these assets such as cost, purchase date, serial number, depreciation, useful economic life, location etc. The total net book value on the fixed asset register must agree to the total net book value in the fixed asset disclosure note.

### 8.3.1    *AUDIT PROCEDURES FOR PLANT, PROPERTY AND EQUIPMENT*

As they are a balance sheet item, the relevant assertions for the auditors to test are:

- Presentation and Disclosure;
- Completeness;
- Ownership (Rights and Obligations);
- Valuation;
- Existence.

## Key risks

Being assets, the main risk for auditors is that these balances are **OVERSTATED**. For example, the company has capitalised assets that it does not own, that do not exist, that are over valued.

Careful attention needs to be paid to **Ownership, Existence and Valuation** (although auditors will still test Presentation and Completeness)

| Ownership | For a selection of fixed assets inspect ownership documents such as title deeds (for land), and vehicle registration documents (for motor vehicles) to ensure that the company has legal title to those assets. |
| --- | --- |
| | Select a sample of operating lease agreements and inspect the fixed asset register to ensure these assets have not been capitalised. |
| | Select a sample of assets that are classified under finance leases. Inspect the terms of the lease agreements to ensure that the risks and rewards lie with the company. |
| **Valuation** | Select a sample of additions and agree the cost to a purchase invoice. |
| | Select a sample of re-valued assets and agree the valuation to the valuation report to ensure it is correct. |
| | Assess the independence, experience and qualifications of any external valuation experts used to ensure their work can be relied upon. |
| | Re-compute depreciation charge for a selection of assets and compare to the company's charge to ensure no material difference. |
| | Inspect fixed asset register for evidence of profits and losses on disposal of assets which may indicate that the depreciation policy chosen is inappropriate. |
| | Inspect fixed asset for evidence of assets with zero net book value that are still in use. This suggests that depreciation policy is inappropriate. |
| | Compare depreciation policy to that used by similar companies in the same industry to ensure they are reasonable. |
| **Existence** | Select a sample of fixed assets from the register and physically verify that they exist. |
| | Inspect a sample of purchase invoices relating to PPE expenditure. Review the invoices for evidence of general repairs and maintenance charges and ensure that these have been recorded on the purchase ledger and not the fixed asset register. |
| **Presentation and Disclosure** | Review the non-current asset disclosure note in the Financial Statements to ensure it meets the criteria set out in IAS 16, Plant Property and Equipment. |
| | Agree the total net book value in the PPE disclosure not to the balance of PPE on the balance sheet to ensure that PPE has been presented net of accumulated depreciation. |
| **Completeness** | Select a sample of assets that physically exist and trace them back to the fixed asset register to ensure that they have been recorded. |
| | Cast the fixed asset register then agree the total net book value on the fixed asset register to the total net book value in the fixed asset disclosure note to ensure that all assets have been included on the balance sheet. |

## 8.4    INTANGIBLE NON-CURRENT ASSETS

The key risks in relation to intangible non-current assets are **valuation** (particularly difficult area for intangibles) and **existence** (should it be recognised as an asset at all?).

| | |
|---|---|
| **Goodwill** | • Agree the cost of the acquisition to the sales agreement.<br><br>• Re-perform the goodwill calculation and compare to client's to ensure it is accurate. |
| **Patents, Copyrights and Licences** | • Agree the valuation of patents and copyrights etc to legal documentation or specialist valuation reports. |
| **Development Costs** | • Inspect costing schedules for capitalised development costs to ensure no research costs have been included.<br><br>• Inspect board meeting minutes for evidence that the company intends to complete the development project.<br><br>• Inspect forecast budgets for development programmes to ensure that income is likely to exceed costs for the products being developed.<br><br>• Inspect prototypes to confirm product exists and appears to work.<br><br>• Inspect market research reports/industry journals for evidence that the product is likely to sell. |

# Exam Question: Simons

You have been asked to carry out the audit of the non current assets of Simons Engineering Limited for the year end 31 March. The draft accounts show the following movements on non-current assets in the year:

| | Freehold Land and Buildings $ | Plant and Machinery $ | Motor Vehicles $ | Total $ |
|---|---|---|---|---|
| **Cost or valuation** | | | | |
| At beginning of year | 353,000 | 406,000 | 173,000 | 932,000 |
| Additions | 292,000 | 86,000 | 65,000 | 443,000 |
| Disposals | - | (29,000) | (47,000) | (76,000) |
| **At end of year** | **645,000** | **463,000** | **191,000** | **1,229,000** |
| **Depreciation** | | | | |
| At beginning of year | 132,000 | 187,000 | 74,000 | 393,000 |
| Charge for year | 12,900 | 43,000 | 42,000 | 97,000 |
| On disposals | - | (25,000) | (32,000) | (57,000) |
| **At end of year** | **144,900** | **205,000** | **84,000** | **433,000** |
| **Net book value at end of year** | **500,000** | **285,000** | **107,000** | **865,000** |

During the current year, the company purchased some land and built a new factory, which was completed during the year.

The company maintains a fixed asset register for all fixed assets, and it depreciates its fixed assets at the following rates:

| | |
|---|---|
| Land and buildings | 2% on cost |
| Plant and machinery | 10% on cost |
| Motor vehicles | 25% on cost |

It is the company's policy to charge a full year's depreciation on assets in the year of purchase and none in the year of disposal.

**Required**

List and describe the audit tests you would perform to verify the amounts shown in fixed assets in the company's accounts for the current year ended 31 March.

**15 marks**

London
School of Business
& Finance

shaping success in business and finance

# Exam Question: Debrief

With 15 marks available you need 15 audit tests, assuming one mark each for a **well-explained** audit test.

An audit test should always have an **objective** i.e. what are you trying to achieve by that test? It is no use saying 'cast the fixed asset register' we 'cast the fixed asset register **to ensure the total net book value is accurate and agrees to the balance in the Financial Statements'.**

There are three categories of asset so you need to think of five tests for each category. Don't forget you can use the mnemonics PROVE and AEIOU to help you to generate ideas.

## Land and Buildings

- **Presentation and Disclosure**: Review the non-current asset disclosure note for land and buildings to ensure the depreciation policy is reasonable (in fact land should not be depreciated at all so this note should be amended in that respect).
- **Records (must be complete and accurate)**: Cast the balance of land and buildings on the fixed asset register and agree the total net book value to the net book value disclosed in the PPE table.
- **Ownership**: Inspect the land registry records for the land purchased during the year and ensure it is in Simon's name.
- **Valuation**: Agree the cost of the land purchased during the year to the sales agreement approved by the solicitors acting for the company to ensure it is recorded at the correct value.
- **Existence**: Select a sample of buildings from the fixed asset register and physically verify them to ensure they actually exist.

## Plant and Machinery

- **Analytical Review**: Compare Simon's depreciation policy for a sample of machinery to the depreciation policy used by other companies in the same industry to ensure it is reasonable. Investigate any significant difference.
- **Enquire** as to any problems or delays to production during the year, as this may indicate a potential impairment of one of the machines.
- Select a sample of plant and machinery additions during the year and **inspect** the purchase invoice to ensure the cost has been recorded correctly.
- **Observe** the plant and machinery while in use in the factory to identify possible slow running or damaged machinery which may need to be impaired.
- **Re-compute** the depreciation charge on a sample of machines and compare to the client's charge to ensure it is reasonable.

## Motor Vehicles

- Select a sample of motor vehicles from the fixed asset register and agree them to the motor vehicle registration documents to ensure that Simon's **owns** them.
- **Re-compute** the profit or loss on disposal of a selection of motor vehicles and compare to the client's calculation to ensure it is accurate.
- **Enquire** of management as to whether or not they hold any cars under operating lease. Ensure these cars are not included on the fixed asset register.
- Agree the cost for a sample of additions to purchase invoices/finance lease agreements to ensure **valuation** is correct.
- **Inspect** insurance claims during the year for evidence of potential impairments to the motor vehicles.

## Learning Summary

- Review the audit procedures in this chapter.
- Watch the video clip 'substantive testing'.
- Attempt the exam question 'Simons'.
- Read the ACCA student article 'Examining Evidence'
  **http://www.accaglobal.com/students/publications/student_accountant/archive/2007/72/2851073**

London
School of Business
& Finance

shaping success in business and finance

9

Receivables

# Context

For most companies, receivables will be a material balance in the Financial Statements. Auditors will spend a good deal of time following audit procedures confirming the receivables balance. These procedures will focus on confirming that the receivables actually exist and that the debts are due to the company. The auditor will check that the receivables have been recorded in the correct period. Testing will also seek to confirm that the receivables have been correctly valued. One standard test that covers a lot of these objectives is the 'receivables circularisation'.

# Exam Hints

Receivables are examined very frequently in the F8 exam, so it is very important that you are fully aware of the standard tests in this area and how to apply them to the scenarios.

A question was asked in December 2007 Q4 (a) that asked students to explain audit procedures using audit software on the receivables balance [9 marks]. Marks were given for tests that should be carried out on the receivables balance and that used a computer to test them (e.g. selecting a sample).

# Key Learning Points

- Receivables confirmations are a key audit test, auditors contact the customers directly to confirm balances.
- Auditors follow up any unconfirmed balances and try to test them another way.
- Testing must establish correct valuation of receivables; this is usually done by testing the appropriateness of the bad debt provision.

# Chapter Overview

This chapter describes the substantive audit procedures for trade receivables.

# 9. Receivables

## 9.1 THE FINANCIAL REPORTING

Receivables are presented in the balance sheet under the heading of 'current assets'. They are presented net of any provision for bad and doubtful debts.

## 9.2 AUDIT PROCEDURES FOR RECEIVABLES

As they are a balance sheet item, the relevant assertions for the auditors to test are:

- Presentation and Disclosure.
- Completeness.
- Ownership (Rights and Obligations).
- Valuation.
- Existence.

### Key Risks

The main risk with regards to receivables is that these balances are **OVERSTATED**. For example, the company may be recognising debts that will never be paid, debts that are disputed by the customer or debts that simply do not exist.

Careful attention needs to be paid to **Existence, Valuation and Ownership** (although, as with PPE, auditors will still test for Presentation and Completeness).

## 9.3 EXISTENCE RECEIVABLES CONFIRMATIONS

The receivables balance will be listed out in detail on the receivables listing which will show each individual debtor's balance. In order for the auditor to check the existence of receivables, they choose a sample of receivables from this list. The client then writes to the debtors that have been chosen asking them to confirm their balance. This is known as a receivables confirmation.

### 9.3.1    HOW CONFIRMATIONS WORK

Letter on
client's paper

Reply sent to
auditor

Positive
method of
confirmation

---

BIG INDUSTRY COMPANY
HIGH ROAD
NEWTOWN

DATE

Dear Sir/Madam

Our auditors request that you would please confirm to them directly that you owe us an amount of £.......... as at (insert date).

If the amount shown above is in agreement with your records, please sign the tear-off slip below and return it to the auditors using the stamped addressed envelope provided.

If this amount is incorrect, please indicate any discrepancies on the reverse of this letter, highlighting any specific differences.

Yours faithfully

J Johnson

Financial Director
Big Industry Co

...........................................................................................

The amount shown above is correct/incorrect* as at (date)

Account number ...................          Signature .....................
Dated .....................

*Please include more information overleaf

---

### 9.3.2    POSITIVE AND NEGATIVE CONFIRMATIONS

A positive confirmation asks the customer to write back if they agree or disagree with the balance

A negative confirmation asks customers to write back only if they disagree. This is not as effective as a positive confirmation as the auditor may assume no response from the customer is an agreement where as the client may have forgotten to reply or never received the letter in the post.

### 9.4    OTHER PROCEDURES

Valuation will focus on whether or not the debts are recoverable and whether or not the bad debt provision is adequate. Ownership will focus on whether or not the company has legal title to the debts. Testing completeness is to ensure that all receivables have been recorded and testing presentation ensures that the correct disclosure has been made in the Financial Statements.

## 9.4  OTHER PROCEDURES

Valuation will focus on whether or not the debts are recoverable and whether or not the bad debt provision is adequate. Ownership will focus on whether or not the company has legal title to the debts. Testing completeness is to ensure that all receivables have been recorded and testing presentation ensures that the correct disclosure has been made in the Financial Statements.

| | |
|---|---|
| **Valuation** | Select a sample of year end receivable balances and trace payment to the post year end cash book to ensure the cash has been received. |
| | Calculate trade receivable days as at the end of each month throughout the year and investigate any significant increase. |
| | Obtain an aged receivables listing and investigate any amounts over 90 days old (say). Enquire as to what management are doing to chase the debts and whether or not they have been provided for. |
| | Inspect legal correspondence with problem customers to ascertain whether or not the company will recover the cash. |
| | Recalculate the bad debt provision and compare it to the client's provision to ensure it is accurate. |
| | Compare the bad debt provision to the actual level of bad debts after the year end to ensure that it is adequate. |
| **Ownership** | Select a sample of receivables and trace to the relevant sales invoice. Ensure that our company (not another company in the group) is the selling company and has the rights to the receivables. |
| **Completeness** | Trace a sample of unpaid sales invoices back to the receivables listing to ensure all credit sales have been recorded. |
| **Presentation** | Review the presentation of receivables in the balance sheet to ensure it has been presented net of the bad debt provision. |

## 9.5  CUT OFF TESTING FOR SALES

The receivables balance is closely related to the sales balance because any sales made on credit will form part of the same double entry. Testing receivables therefore links to the testing of sales.

A key risk with sales is that they are overstated and one common way to illegally manipulate sales is to incorrectly treat the sales around the year end for example, taking sales from early in the next year and pretending that they were made before the year end.

IAS 18 Revenue, says that a sale should be recorded when the goods are delivered to the customer. To check that the sales are being recorded, the auditor will:

- select a sample of **goods despatch notes dated before the year end** and trace the sale to the receivables ledger and the sales ledger and ensure the goods have been excluded from stock;
- select a sample of goods despatch notes from just after the year end and verify that the sale is excluded from the year end receivables and sales ledger and that the goods are in year end stock.

# Learning Example 1

Suggest indicators that would indicate that a finance director may have to make a bad debt provision for a specific debtor?

# Exam Question: Sherwood

Sherwood Textiles manufactures knitted clothes and dyes these clothes and other textiles. You are carrying out the audit of the accounts of the company for the year ended 31 March, which shows a turnover of about $10 million, a profit before tax of about $800,000.

You are attending the final audit in June and are commencing the audit of trade receivables, which are shown in the draft accounts at $2,060,000.

The interim audit (i.e. controls testing) was carried out in February and it showed that there was a good system of internal control in the sales system, as no serious errors were found in the control test.

The company sales ledger is maintained on a computer, which produces at the end of each month:

(i)   a list of transactions for the month;

(ii)  an aged list of balances; and

(iii) customer statements.

## Required

(a) List and briefly describe the audit test you would carry out to verify trade receivables at the year end – you are not required to describe how you would carry out a debtors circularization.

(10 marks)

(b) Explain the difference between positive and negative circularisation.

(2 marks)

(c) Describe the audit work you would carry out on the following replies to a positive circularisation:

(i)   Balance agreed by debtor.

(2 marks)

(ii)  Balance not agreed by debtor.

(3 marks)

(iii) Debtor does not reply to the circularization.

(3 marks)

**(Total 20 marks)**

## Solution to Learning Example 1

Customers who have very old debt on the ledger – they may have forgotten to pay, or may be disputing the amount.

Customers who have not made any payments on their accounts for a very long time – again, they many have forgotten to pay, may be struggling to pay or may be disputing the amount.

Customers who have made payments relating to recent invoices but who have aged invoices that they have not paid – the old invoices may be in dispute, or may not be genuine.

A customer that is disputing invoices – they may be dissatisfied and unwilling to pay.

Any customers who have made a high number of goods returns – they may also be dissatisfied and unwilling to pay.

Signs that one of the customers is in financial difficulty – they may be unable to meet the payment terms.

Customers who are asking for increases in their credit limit – they may have cash flow difficulties and may be struggling to pay.

## Exam Question: Debrief

PART A)

There are 10 marks available so you will need you need 10 audit tests, assuming one mark each for a **well-explained** audit test.

Don't forget you can use the mnemonics PROVE and AEIOU to help you to generate ideas.

| | |
|---|---|
| **Presentation** | Review the presentation of receivables in the balance sheet to ensure it has been presented net of the bad debt provision debtors ledger, *or*<br><br>Inspect the trade receivables ledger for credit balances that should be presented as liabilities and not receivables. |
| **Records (Complete and Accurate)** | Select a sample of pre year end goods despatch notes and trace the transaction to the receivables ledger to ensure that pre year end receivables are complete. |
| **Ownership** | Select a sample of receivables and trace to the relevant sales invoice. Ensure that our company (not another company in the group) is the selling company and has the rights to the receivables. |
| **Valuation** | Select a sample of trade receivables and inspect the post year end bank statements for evidence that these customers have paid. |
| **Existence** | Select a sample of trade receivables for circularisation to ensure that these receivables exist. |

| | |
|---|---|
| **Analytical Review** | Calculate trade receivable days at each month end. A significant increase may suggest that some debts are bad. |
| **Enquiry** | Ask the credit control department what measures they are taking to chase bad debts and if there are any problem customers whose debts may need to be written off. |
| **Inspection** | Inspect the aged debtors listing and trace any over 90 days old to the bad debt provision to ensure that have been provided for. |
| **Observation** | Observe credit control staff calling problem debtors to ensure that the company is taking steps recover bad debts. |
| **CompUte** | Recalculate the bad debt provision and compare it to the client's figure to ensure it is reasonable. |

PART B)

### Positive Confirmation

A positive confirmation requires the customer to write back if they agree or disagree with the balance.

### Negative Confirmation

A negative confirmation requires the customer to write back only if they disagree.

This is not as effective as a positive confirmation as the auditor may assume no response from the customer is an agreement where as the customer may have forgotten to reply or never received the letter in the post.

PART C)

### Audit Work when Balance Agreed by Customer

- Call customer to check that the employee who agreed the balance was authorised to do so.
- Double check the agreed balance to the ledger.

### Audit Work when Balance Not Agreed by Customer

- Call customer to reconcile the differences.
- Agree balance to internal records such as GDNs and invoices.

### Audit Work when Customer Does Not Respond

- Write again or telephone to try to get agreement.
- If still no response, inspect bank statement for evidence that the customer has paid the balance after the year end.

## Learning Summary

- Review the audit tests suggested in this chapter.
- Watch the video clip on 'Substantive Testing'.
- Attempt the exam question 'Sherwood'.

London
School of Business
& Finance

shaping success in business and finance

# 10

## Inventories

London
School of Business
& Finance

shaping success in business and finance

# Context

For most companies, inventory will be a material balance in the Financial Statements. Auditors will spend a good deal of time following audit procedures to confirm the inventory balance. These procedures will focus mainly on confirming that the inventories actually exist and that they are valued correctly. Attending the client's inventory count will be an important aspect of this work.

# Exam Hints

Substantive audit procedures for inventories are examined frequently in F8. In December 2007 students were asked to detail both a control test and a substantive test that auditors would carry out during the inventory count.

# Key Learning Points

- Where opening and closing Work In Progress (WIP) occurs we need to identify how much 'work' has been performed on units of production. The concept of Equivalent Units (EU) is used where:

  o the main risk with regards to inventories is overstatement of the balance. Auditors will focus on audit procedures to test existence and valuation;

  o where clients have a material inventory balance, ISAs require auditors to attend the inventory count.

# Chapter Overview

This chapter describes the substantive audit procedures for inventories.

## 10. Inventories

### 10.1 THE FINANCIAL REPORTING

Inventories are presented in the balance sheet under 'current assets'. They are valued at the lower of cost and net realisable value.

### 10.2 AUDIT PROCEDURES FOR INVENTORIES

The relevant assertions to test for inventories are:

- Presentation and Disclosure.
- Completeness.
- Ownership (Rights and Obligations).
- Valuation.
- Existence.

**Key Risks**

The main risk with regards to inventories is that these balances are **OVERSTATED**. For example, the company may be recognising inventory that is obsolete, damaged, that does not belong to them or does not exist.

Careful attention needs to be paid to **Existence, Valuation and Ownership** (although, as with all balance sheet items, auditors will still test for Presentation and Completeness).

### 10.3 THE INVENTORY COUNT

The ISAs require auditors to attend the client's inventory count in cases where inventory is a material balance in the Financial Statements.

It is important for the exam that you know about the audit procedures *before, during* and *after* the inventory count.

#### 10.3.1 BEFORE THE INVENTORY COUNT (PLANNING)

- Speak to the client about logistics such as date, time and location of the inventory count.
- Ask the client for a copy of the inventory count instructions that will be given to the client's staff. Review them to ensure they are adequate.
- Ask the client how they propose to deal with problem areas such as WIP (work in progress) and consignment stock (that belongs to third parties).
- Timetable a member of the audit team to attend the stock count and give them instructions.
- Review the prior year working papers for evidence of any problems.

#### 10.3.2 DURING THE INVENTORY COUNT

- Observe the client's staff following the inventory count instructions.
- Inspect the stock sheets to ensure they are sequentially numbered.
- Confirm by observation that inventory is labelled as it is counted so as not to be counted again.
- Perform some test counts:
    o select a number of items from the stock sheets and recount these to ensure that they physically exist;
    o select a number of actual stock items and trace them to the count sheets to ensure the stock records are complete.
- Look out for, and make a note of, damaged, obsolete and slow moving stock (e.g. look out for physical damage, items covered in dust, items past their sell by date).
- Confirm that consignment stock is separately identified and not included in the count.
- Come to a conclusion as to whether the count has been properly carried out.

10.3.3 *AFTER THE INVENTORY COUNT*

- Agree the balance of items on the inventory count sheets to the final inventory listing.
- Ensure that any damaged or obsolete items noted have been considered during the valuation exercise.
- Perform some cut-off testing on sales and purchases of stock:
  - o select a sample of goods despatch notes dated before the year end and inspect the stock records to ensure that the items have been excluded from year end stock;
  - o select a sample of goods despatch notes from just after the year end trace the goods to the stock records to ensure they have been included at the year end;
  - o select a sample of goods received notes dated before the year end and trace the goods to the stock records to ensure they have been included at the year end;
  - o select a sample of goods received notes dated after the year end and inspect the stock records to ensure the items have been excluded from year end stock.

## 10.4    OTHER PROCEDURES

| Valuation | For a sample of raw materials, agree cost back to purchase invoices. |
| --- | --- |
| | For a sample of finished goods held at the year end, inspect post year end sales invoices to ensure that the sales price was greater than cost. |
| | Obtain the costing records for a sample of WIP and: |
| | • agree labour costs to payroll; |
| | • agree labour hours to time sheets; |
| | • recalculate the overhead absorption rate. |
| | Obtain the aged inventory analysis and ensure older items have been written off. |
| | Calculate inventory days as at each month end throughout the year and investigate any significant increases. |
| **Ownership** | Select a sample of consignment stock agreements and inspect the inventory records to ensure these items have not been included in the inventory records. |
| **Completeness and Existence** | Agree the figures from the inventory records tested at the inventory count to the final inventory figures in the Financial Statements. |
| **Presentation** | Review the presentation of inventories in the balance sheet to ensure that balances of raw materials, work in progress and finished goods have been disclosed separately. |

# Learning Example 1

State which types of inventory may be worth less than cost and describe the investigations you would carry out to identify this stock.

## Solution to Learning Example 1

*Inventories that may be worth less than cost:*

- Damaged items.
- Obsolete items.
- Custom built items but the customer has since cancelled the order.

*How to identify these inventories:*

Calculate inventory holding days for each month of the year. An increase may suggest slow moving inventories.

Inspect items in the warehouse for signs of damage.

Inspect a number of credit notes issued during the year to ascertain the level of faulty items being returned by customers.

Inspect the aged inventory analysis and investigate any old stock.

Review Board meeting minutes for evidence of any production problems during the year which may be due to faulty raw materials.

## Learning Summary

- Review the audit tests suggested in this chapter.
- Watch the video clip on 'Substantive Testing'.

London
School of Business
& Finance

shaping success in business and finance

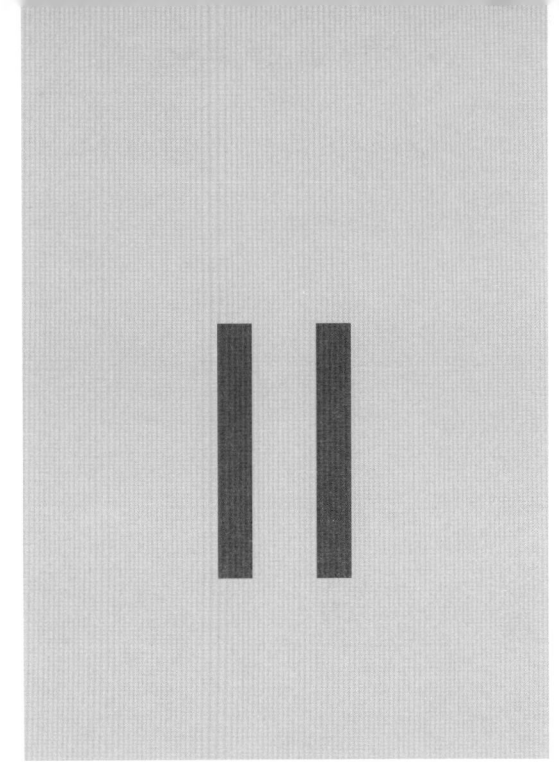

# Trade Payables and Other Liabilities

# Context

Companies often have a much wider variety of liabilities than they have receivables including balances such as trade payables, payroll liabilities, tax liabilities, long-term loans and provisions. The main risk with regards to liabilities in understatement so this makes for a tricky area for the auditor – they may have to spend time looking for balances that the company is deliberately trying to hide. Auditors will therefore focus many of their procedures on testing whether liabilities are complete.

# Exam Hints

In December 2008 students were required to describe audit procedures they would carry out on the purchases and trade payables system. This was part of the long 30-mark scenario question.

# Key Learning Points

- Testing for completeness is key when auditing any liability.
- Using analytical procedures such as calculating trade payable days can be a useful way of spotting unusual movements and potential understatement in the trade payables balance.
- Cut off testing can be used to ensure that purchases made just before and after the year end have been recorded in the correct period.

# Chapter Overview

This chapter describes the substantive audit procedures for trade payables and other liabilities.

# 11. Trade Payables and other Liabilities

11.1    THE FINANCIAL REPORTING

Trade payables are presented under 'current liabilities' in the balance sheet.

11.2    AUDIT PROCEDURES FOR TRADE PAYABLES

As they are a balance sheet item, the relevant assertions for the auditors to test are:

*   Presentation and Disclosure.
*   Completeness.
*   Ownership (Rights and Obligations).
*   Valuation.
*   Existence.

### Key risks

The main risk with regards to payables is that these balances are **UNDERSTATED**. For example the company may have accidentally or deliberately failed to record certain liabilities in order for the balance sheet to look stronger.

Careful attention needs to be paid to completeness and cut-off to ensure that all credit purchases made just before the year end have been captured.

| Completeness | <ul><li>Calculate trade payable days for each month of the year. A significant decrease may indicate understatement of trade payables.</li><li>Compare the list of supplier balances with the previous year and seek explanations for any suppliers that are missing this year.</li><li>Review the bank statement for post year end payments by the company and trace to supporting documentation. If they relate to pre-year end purchases, there should be a payable recorded in the year end ledger</li><li>For a sample of supplier statements received, agree the balance owed per the supplier to the balance owed per the client's ledger and investigate any differences</li><li>Perform cut off testing – see below</li><li>Compare the list of accruals with prior year and investigate any accruals that are missing this year.</li><li>Review the bank statement for post year end payments that may relate to services used before the year end. Trace these items to the accruals listing.</li></ul> |
|---|---|
| Valuation | <ul><li>Perform a payables circularisation for a sample of suppliers requesting confirmation that they agree with the balance (although this is rare in practice)</li></ul> |

11.3    CUT OFF TESTING FOR PURCHASES

The trade payables balance is closely related to the purchases balance because any purchases made on credit will form part of the same double entry. Testing trade payables therefore links to the testing of purchases.

A key risk with purchases is that they are understated and one common way to illegally manipulate purchases is to incorrectly treat the purchases around the year end for example, taking purchases from shortly before the year end and recording them in next year's accounts.

London
School of Business
& Finance

shaping success in business and finance

A purchase should be recorded when the goods are received. To check that the purchases are being recorded in the correct period, the auditor will:

- Select a sample of **goods received notes dated before the year end** and trace the purchase to the purchases ledger and the payables ledger and ensure the goods have been included from stock.
- Select a sample of goods received notes from just after the year end and verify that the purchase is excluded from the year end trade payables ledger and the purchases ledger and that the goods are excluded from year end stock.

## 11.4    OTHER LIABILITIES

Companies often have a much wider variety of liabilities than they have receivables including balances such as payroll liabilities, tax liabilities, long-term loans and provisions.

| | |
|---|---|
| **Payroll** | Agree payroll liability in the balance sheet back to the year end payroll records. |
| | Agree payment of net pay as per the payroll records to the bank statement. |
| | Agree the payment of employers taxes as per the payroll records to the bank statement. |
| | Agree a sample of individual wages back to records such as employment contracts or timesheet records. |
| **Corporation Tax** | Agree the year end tax liability back to the year end tax computation. |
| | Agree the year end tax liability to the post year end payment to the tax authorities. |
| | Agree the corporation tax liability to the amount owed as per correspondence from the  tax authorities. |
| **Long-Term Loans** | Agree loan balances back to the loan statement from the bank. |
| | Inspect the bank confirmation letter for details of loans and overdrafts and trace these amounts to the balance sheet to ensure they have been recorded. |
| | Review Board minutes for evidence of new loans being taken out in the year and ensure they have been recorded. |
| | Inspect the bank statements for the year for evidence of a significant deposit, which may be proceeds of a loan. |
| | Recalculate expected interest charges during the year and compare to the client's figure. |

Audit procedures for provisions are discussed in chapter 4.

# Learning Example 1

Your client Marley Ltd has the following balances for trade payables and provisions.  Describe the audit tests you would carry out to ensure that the balances are fairly stated.

| | $'000 | $'000 |
|---|---|---|
| Trade payables | 426 | 789 |
| Provisions | 525 | - |

The provision relates to legal action brought by a competitor who says that Marley have illegally copied the design of their best selling product.

## Solution to Learning Example 1

### Trade Payables

- Calculate trade payable days for each month end and follow up any significant movement. A decrease may suggest that payables are understated.
- Compare the list of supplier balances with the previous year and seek explanations for any suppliers that are missing this year.
- Review the bank statement for post year end payments by the company and trace to supporting documentation. If they relate to pre-year end purchases, there should be a payable recorded in the year end ledger.
- For a sample of supplier statements received, agree the balance owed per the supplier to the balance owed per the client's ledger and investigate any differences.
- Select a sample of goods received notes dated before the year end and trace the purchase to the purchases ledger and the payables ledger.

### Provision

- Obtain a breakdown of potential damages and costs by inspecting correspondence from the company's lawyers and compare these to the client's provision to ensure it is adequate.
- Inspect post year end court documents and lawyers correspondence for evidence of the case being settled post year end and if the actual costs were in line with the provision?
- Inspect correspondence with the company's lawyers to get a feel for the likelihood of losing the case in order to decide whether it is correct to recognise a provision or whether a contingent liability should be recognised instead.
- Review trade journals and the press to find evidence of similar cases and the potential outcome.

## Learning summary

- Review the audit tests suggested in this chapter.
- Watch the video clip on 'Substantive Testing'.

# 12

# Bank and Cash

# Context

Cash is an important area for the auditor. Not only is there a higher risk of fraud and misappropriation when dealing with cash, but also a lack of cash can signal going concern problems for a company. Auditors will need to focus on both the existence of the positive cash balances and the completeness of overdrafts and loans. The bank confirmation letter is an effective way of proving existence, completeness and ownership of cash.

# Exam Hints

Substantive audit procedures will mainly be examined in the long 30-mark scenario question. Students must be comfortable with generating substantive procedures for the main balances in the Financial Statements.

# Key Learning Points

- The bank confirmation letter is a key audit test over the existence, valuation and ownership of cash. It details the balances held by the company and also any overdrafts and loans so it can also be used to test the completeness of liabilities.

# Chapter Overview

This chapter describes the substantive audit procedures for cash and bank balances.

## 12. Bank and Cash

12.1   THE FINANCIAL REPORTING

Positive cash balances are presented under current assets.  Negative cash balances (i.e. overdrafts) should not be offset against positive balances but are instead disclosed separately under 'current liabilities'.

12.2   AUDIT PROCEDURES FOR BANK AND CASH

As they are a balance sheet item, the relevant assertions for the auditors to test are:

- Presentation and Disclosure;
- Completeness;
- Ownership (Rights and Obligations);
- Valuation;
- Existence.

### Key risks

The main risk with regards bank and cash is that positive balances are **OVERSTATED** and overdrafts are **UNDERSTATED**.  Positive balances need to be tested carefully for **existence** and **ownership** and for overdrafts, particular attention needs to be paid to **completeness**.

12.3   THE BANK CONFIRMATION LETTER

The bank confirmation letter is an effective way of proving existence, completeness, valuation and ownership of cash.

The auditor writes to the company's bankers to request details of balances and other information (such as loans and guarantees) so that this can be agreed to the client's records. This is a valuable form of audit evidence as it comes from an **independent** source.

London
School of Business
& Finance
shaping success in business and finance

12.3.1  *EXAMPLE OF THE INFORMATION REQUESTED*

---

BIG BUCKS BANK PLC

DATE

Dear Sir/Madam

We are writing to request disclosure of the following information for our mutual client:

### Account and Balance Details

Give full details of all bank accounts and loans

State if any accounts are subject to restrictions

### Facilities

Give the following details of all loans, overdrafts and guarantees:

Term
Repayments
Availability of finance
Limit of the facility

### Charges

Does the bank hold a fixed or floating charge over any of the company's assets and if so give details

### Additional Banking Relationships

Does the client have any additional relationships with branches or subsidiaries of the bank that have not been mentioned above?


*A Audit Partner*


Partner
Audit Co

---

## 12.4 OTHER PROCEDURES

- Agree balances to year end bank statements.
- Obtain the year end bank reconciliation:
  - o cast it;
  - o agree the 'balance per cash book' to the cash book;
  - o agree the 'balance per bank statement' to the bank statement;
  - o trace the reconciling items to the post year end bank statement to ensure they have cleared in a timely manner.
- For any accounts in a foreign currency, re-perform the translation of the balance at the year end using an exchange rate from an independent source (e.g. the Financial Times) and compare this to the client's translation.
- Recount a sample of petty cash tins and agree the balance to records.

# Learning Example 1

Describe four matters which may be covered in a bank letter and explain why they are important for the auditor.

London
School of Business
& Finance

shaping success in business and finance

## Solution to Learning Example 1

| Matter | Why it is important to the auditor |
| --- | --- |
| Balances of any accounts held | To substantiate the balance of cash and overdrafts in the balance sheet. |
| Overdraft facility | To understand how much short term finance is available to the company should they run short of cash. |
| Bank Loans | To support the balance of liabilities on the balance sheet. |
| Charges | To understand if bank has any charges over the company's assets as these will need to be disclosed in the Financial Statements. |

## Learning Summary

- Review the audit tests in this chapter.
- Watch the video clip 'substantive testing'.

# 13

# Auditing in a
# Computer
# Environment

# Context

The fundamental aspects of an audit do not change when the audit is carried out in a computer environment although the auditor will make use of Computer Assisted Audit Techniques (CAATs) to assist in gathering evidence.  CAATs can be used to test controls and to perform substantive testing.

# Exam Hints

Computer assisted audit techniques are often examined as part of a scenario question. The examiner often asks students to explain how CAATs can be used in order to test the controls in a particular system or a particular balance so it is important to be able to apply knowledge of CAATs to practical situations.

In December 2007 students were asked to describe the audit procedures for trade receivables that would be carried out using audit software.

# Key Learning Points

- There are two main types of Computer Assisted Audit Techniques; test data and audit software.
- Test data is used to test controls. The auditors input data into the client's system to check that it is processed as expected.
- Audit software helps the auditors to perform substantive procedures.  It will carry out tasks such as sampling, analytical procedures and casting.

# Chapter Overview

This chapter describes:

- Computer controls;
- Computer Assisted Audit Techniques;
    - o  test data; and
    - o  audit software.

# 13. Auditing in a Computer Environment

## 13.1 COMPUTER CONTROLS

There are two main types of controls that a client may have in operation over their IT systems:

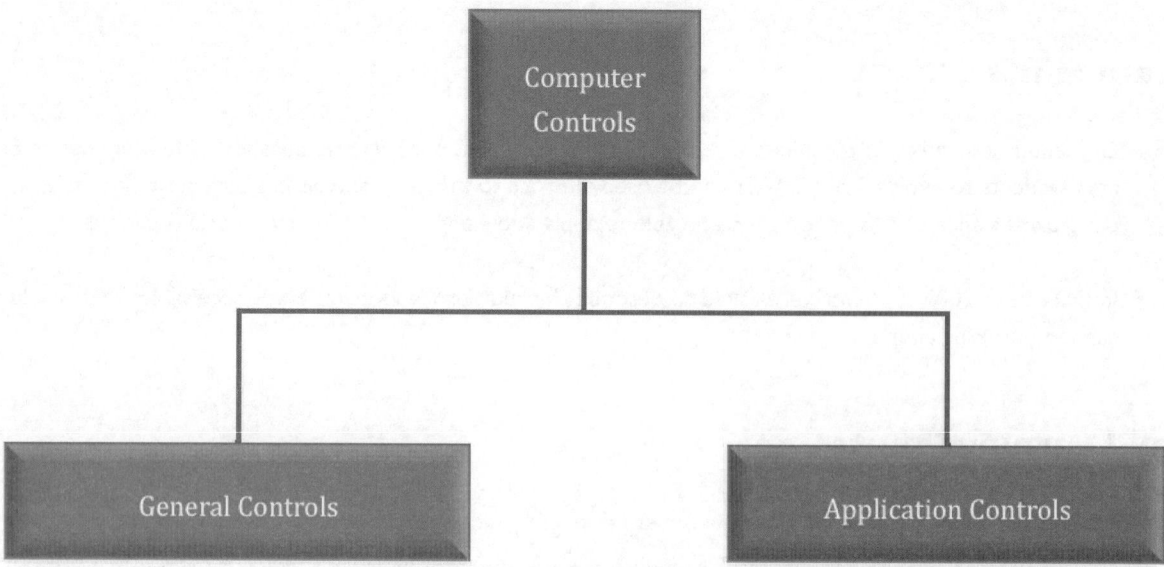

### 13.1.1 GENERAL CONTROLS

General controls cover the *computer environment as a whole*. Examples include:

- making regular back-ups of data and storing them off-site;
- having an IT help-desk and IT training for staff;
- keeping computers in locked rooms;
- having a disaster recovery plan;
- all computers have log in codes;
- anti-virus soft ware and firewalls;
- segregation of duties between programmers and users.

### 13.1.2 APPLICATION CONTROLS

Application controls are the controls over data in *specific computer programmes*. Application controls are needed to ensure that all transactions are authorised, recorded and processed accurately so they should cover the input, processing and output of data as well as the **standing data** on the system.

**Standing Data**

Standing data is the information that is held on computer files for long-term use. It is called standing data as it tends to change less frequently than other data.

Examples of standing data would be:

- the rate of sales tax to be applied to sales invoices;
- the hourly pay rate for a factory worker to be used when calculating payroll;
- employee bank account details.

Examples of application controls include:

- passwords;
- exception reports;
- one to one checking of inputs;
- batch checking of inputs;
- reasonableness tests (e.g. sales tax to total value);
- character checks (e.g. no unexpected characters entered);
- range limits (e.g. no transaction processes over or under a certain value);
- manual checks to ensure input was authorised;
- print outs and checks of amendments to standing data.

## 13.2 COMPUTER ASSISTED AUDIT TECHNIQUES (CAATS)

Auditors can use computers and computer software to assist with the audit process. There are two main types of computer assisted audit techniques, both with different roles in the overall audit process. These are **test data** and **audit software**.

### 13.2.1 TEST DATA

Test data is used to **test controls** within a client's computer system.

When using test data, the auditor invents some data and runs it through the client's system to ensure it is processed as expected.

**Examples Include:**

- The auditor may invent a fake password to try and enter the system and it should be rejected.
- The system may have a range limit so that when processing payroll for example, no employee can have worked more than 70 hours per week. The auditor will try to enter 80 hours and this should be rejected.

However, there are drawbacks to the use of test data:

- Any false transactions must be removed from the system afterwards.
- This may cause inconvenience for the client.

### 13.2.2 AUDIT SOFTWARE

Audit software is used to perform **substantive tests** on client data. The auditor uploads a copy of the client's data onto their own computer and runs it through the audit software, which assists in performing tasks such as:

- reorganising the data into a more useful format e.g. by producing an aged listing for receivables or stock;
- performing detailed analytical procedures (e.g. inventory holding days by stock line);
- checking arithmetic by casting ledgers and lists;
- re-performance of calculations;
- sequence checks;
- choosing random samples.

## 13.2.3 ADVANTAGES AND DISADVANTAGES OF AUDIT SOFTWARE

| Advantages | Disadvantages |
| --- | --- |
| Easy to use. | Expensive to develop especially when the client is new and the system is not fully understood by the auditor or if there is a lack of documentation on the system. |
| Limited IT skills required to use. | Limited to procedures that can be carried out on electronic data. |
| Improves efficiency of audit as large volumes of data can be processed quickly. | Extensive modification required if client changes their systems. |
| Can be used in future audits and for similar clients. | Use of copy files (auditors are checking copies of the client's data and need to be sure that these copies accurately reflect the genuine live data). |

# Learning Example 1

Describe a number of tests you could perform using test data and audit software on a client's sales and receivables ledger files.

# Solution to Learning Example I

### Test Data

- Try to enter the system to record a sale with a fake password to ensure it is rejected.
- Try to enter a sale that breaches the customer's credit limit to ensure it is rejected.
- Try to enter a sale without all of the customer details, e.g. delivery address, to ensure the transaction cannot continue without all of the details.
- Try to enter a sales order without checking stock first to ensure that the system prompts the user to check stock levels before proceeding.
- Enter a sales order with the wrong date (e.g. 12/14/56) to ensure it is rejected.

### Audit Software

- Produce an aged receivables listing so that the older receivables can be investigated.
- Calculate trade receivable days at the end of each month of the year so that significant changes can be followed up.
- Select a sample of trade receivables to be circularised in order to prove their existence.
- Cast the receivables and sales ledgers to ensure the additions are accurate and agree to the totals on the control accounts.
- Re-perform the calculation of sales tax for a sample of sales invoices.
- Extract all of the negative balances from the receivables ledger so they can be moved to liabilities.

# Learning summary

- Watch the video clip 'Auditing in a Computer Environment'.

# 14

## Completion
## and Review

# Context

Before the auditors reach their conclusion on the Financial Statements there are a number of important reviews that need to take place. Of particular concern are the subsequent events and the going concern reviews. Both subsequent events and going concern can have a material impact on the Financial Statements so it is up to the auditors to ensure that the directors have made the correct disclosures with regards to these two areas. If not, there may be consequences for the audit opinion.

# Exam Hints

Both subsequent events and going concern have featured heavily in recent F8 examinations. In both June and December 2008, students were asked to describe procedures that the auditors would undertake in order to ensure the company being audited was still a going concern. In December 2008, students were asked for both the definition and the auditor's responsibility with regards to subsequent events.

# Key Learning Points

- Subsequent events are those that take place between the year end and the date that the financial statements are authorised for issue. There are two types of subsequent event, adjusting and non-adjusting.
- Auditors have an active responsibility to identify subsequent events up until the date that the financial statements are authorised. After that date, auditors do not have an active responsibility with regards to subsequent events, however if they come across one, they must take appropriate action.
- Auditors have a responsibility to consider whether or not it is appropriate for the accounts to be prepared on a going concern basis. If there are doubts over going concern, auditors must ensure that these are adequately disclosed.

# Chapter Overview

This chapter covers:

- final review;
- subsequent events;
- going concern;
- management representations.

# 14. Completion and Review

## 14.1 FINAL REVIEW

It is crucial that auditors carry out a final review of the audit work before forming the audit opinion. The final review should be designed to answer questions such as:

- Has the audit work been performed in accordance with the relevant legal and professional requirements?
- Is the quality of audit work up to standard?
- Are the Financial Statements consistent with our knowledge of the business?
- Have the Financial Statements been prepared in line with relevant accounting and legal requirements?
- Do the Financial Statements give a true and fair view?
- Have significant issues been resolved?

Often auditors will perform analytical procedures as part of this final review. The analytical procedures act as a final sense check on the numbers in the accounts.

## 14.2 SUBSEQUENT EVENTS

Subsequent events are those events occurring between the year end and the date that the Financial Statements are authorised for issue (i.e. signed by the directors) that may affect the numbers or disclosures in the year end Financial Statements.

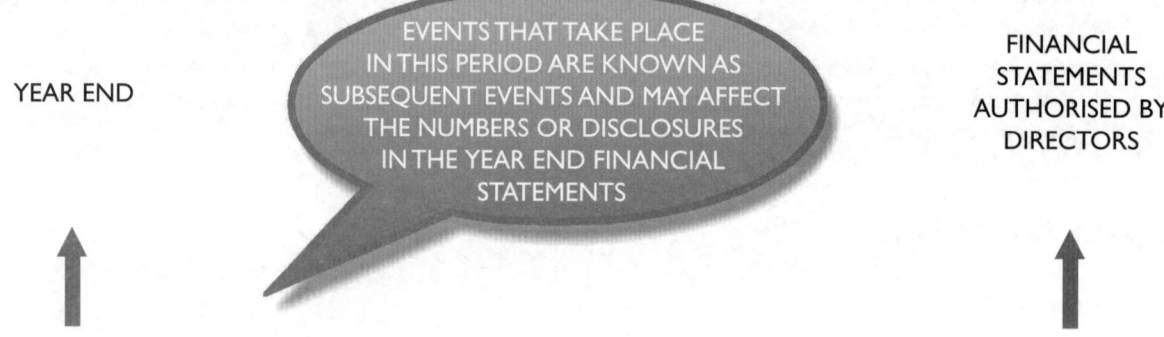

## 14.2.1 *TREATMENT OF SUBSEQUENT EVENTS: A FINANCIAL REPORTING RECAP*

There are two types of subsequent event:

- those that we adjust the year end Financial Statements for: **ADJUSTING EVENTS**;
- those that we do not adjust for: **NON-ADJUSTING EVENTS**.

| ADJUSTING EVENTS | NON-ADJUSTING EVENTS |
|---|---|
| Those that provide evidence of conditions existing at the year end. | Those providing evidence of conditions arising the year end. |
| For example: A company has a receivable in its year end balance sheet but shortly after the year end, this customer goes into liquidation. The liquidation is evidence of the condition of the debt after the year end i.e. it is bad (the customer will have been experiencing difficulties before the year end). | For example: A company has balance of inventory in its year end balance sheet but shortly after the year end, this inventory is destroyed in a fire. The fire is evidence of a condition arising after the year end and in fact the condition of the inventory at the year end is fine. |
| The directors will adjust the year end Financial Statements by writing off the debt. | The directors will not adjust the year end Financial Statements to write off the inventory but will disclose any material non-adjusting events in a note to the Financial Statements. |

14.2.2    *THE AUDITOR'S RESPONSIBILITY WITH REGARDS TO SUBSEQUENT EVENTS*

The auditor has a responsibility to review subsequent events before they sign their audit report and may have to take action if they become aware of subsequent events arising between the date the audit report is signed and the Financial Statements are distributed to shareholders.

The exact responsibilities are shown on the time line below:

| YEAR END | FINANCIAL STATEMENTS AUTHORISED AND AUDIT REPORT SIGNED | FINANCIAL STATEMENTS DISTRIBUTED TO SHAREHOLDERS |
|---|---|---|
|  |  |  |

The auditor should **actively perform audit procedures** to actively identify subsequent events such as:

- enquiries of management as to major events such as customer liquidations, destruction of assets, issue of shares, litigation, going concern problems;
- review meeting minutes for evidence of subsequent events;
- review of press and trade journals for evidence of customer liquidations.

The auditors do not have any responsibility to perform procedures to identify subsequent events but if they come across a subsequent event that may affect the year end Financial Statements, they should:

- consider the effect on the Financial Statements;
- consider the effect on the audit opinion;
- if necessary ask the directors not to distribute the Financial Statements and issue a new audit report.

The auditor should **actively perform audit procedures** to actively identify subsequent events such as:

- enquiries of management as to major events such as customer liquidations, destruction of assets, issue of shares, litigation, going concern problems;
- review meeting minutes for evidence of subsequent events;
- review of press and trade journals for evidence of customer liquidations.

## 14.3    GOING CONCERN

Companies should prepare their accounts on a going concern basis if the company is expected to continue in operation for the foreseeable future.

When preparing the Financial Statements, directors should consider whether or not there are any doubts about the company's ability to continue as a going concern. If there are doubts, these must be disclosed in a note to the Financial Statements.

Auditors have a responsibility to consider whether or not it is appropriate for the accounts to be prepared on a going concern basis. If there are doubts over going concern, auditors must ensure that these are adequately disclosed.

Auditors therefore will need to:

- identify indications of going concern problems;
- apply audit procedures to assess a company's going concern status.

### 14.3.1    INDICATIONS OF GOING CONCERN PROBLEMS

The possibilities are extensive but auditors should look out for potential indicators such as:

- net liabilities;
- operating losses;
- major debt repayments due;
- loss of major customers or suppliers;
- loss of key staff;
- withdrawal of financing such as overdrafts;
- cash flow problems;
- technological advancements causing client's product to become obsolete;
- major litigation.

### 14.3.2    AUDIT PROCEDURES TO ASSESS ABILITY TO CONTINUE AS A GOING CONCERN

The actual procedures that auditors will carry out will vary from client to client depending upon the exact circumstances but will tend to involve procedures such as:

- review and discuss cash-flow forecasts to ensure company has enough cash to continue in operation for the next year.
- review budgets and interim Financial Statements to assess projected results over the next year and identify any concerns over profitability.
- inspect correspondence with the company's bankers to assess the availability of financing such as overdrafts and loans.
- inspect business plans to assess company's efforts to expand into new areas to replace unprofitable operations.
- inspect employee contracts to ensure company is replacing key staff and providing incentives for current staff.
- inspect correspondence to understand possible consequences of legal action being brought against the company.
- inspect new sales contracts to ensure company is replacing customers who have been lost.
- consider management's process for identifying going concern problems and how they propose to respond to those problems.

## 14.4    MANAGEMENT REPRESENTATIONS

The term management representation simply means that the directors 'confirm something to the auditors', usually in response to one of the auditor's queries. They are a form of audit evidence.

The ISAs require auditors to obtain written representations from management on matters material to the Financial Statements where other sufficient, appropriate, audit evidence cannot reasonably be expected to exist.

Matters included in a management representation letter.

### 14.4.1   *GENERAL MATTERS*

Directors confirm that:

*   they are responsible for the Financial Statements;
*   they are responsible for internal controls and for preventing and detecting fraud;
*   the going concern basis is appropriate;
*   all related party transactions have been disclosed;
*   there are no subsequent events that require adjustment or disclosure.

### 14.4.2   *SPECIFIC MATTERS*

Included here is anything else that the auditor would like a representation on for example:

*   that a certain debt is recoverable;
*   all bank accounts have been disclosed;
*   any plans to reorganise the business or discontinue product lines have already been disclosed.

## 14.4    MANAGEMENT REPRESENTATIONS

The term **management representation** simply means that the directors 'confirm something to the auditors', usually in response to one of the auditor's queries. They are a form of audit evidence.

The ISAs require auditors to obtain written representations from management on matters material to the Financial Statements where other sufficient, appropriate, audit evidence cannot reasonably be expected to exist.

**Matters Included in a Management Representation Letter**

### 14.4.1   *GENERAL MATTERS*

Directors confirm that:

*   they are responsible for the Financial Statements;
*   they are responsible for internal controls and for preventing and detecting fraud;
*   the going concern basis is appropriate;
*   there are no subsequent events that require adjustment or disclosure.

### 14.4.2   *SPECIFIC MATTERS*

Included here is anything else that the auditor would like a representation on, for example:

*   that a certain debt is recoverable;
*   all bank accounts have been disclosed;
*   any plans to reorganise the business or discontinue product lines have already been disclosed.

# Learning Summary

*   Read the BBC article 'The importance of going concern'.
    **http://news.bbc.co.uk/1/hi/business/7875661.stm**

15

Audit
Reports

AUDIT AND ASSURANCE

# Context

The final thing for the auditors to do is to pull together all of the evidence and give their opinion on the Financial Statements. This opinion is contained in the audit report. A true and fair opinion with no other issues will lead to an unmodified report. There are, however, certain situations where the auditors may have to modify their opinion or add in an emphasis of matter paragraph.

# Exam Hints

In December 2007 students were asked to describe the meaning and purpose of particular extracts from the audit report. In the same question, they were also presented with an audit problem (the company was refusing to depreciate some of its non-current assets) and were asked what the effect on the audit report would be.

# Key Learning Points

- All audit reports follow a basic format, which is prescribed by the ISAs.
- An audit report may be modified either by changing the audit opinion or by adding an emphasis of matter paragraph.
- If there is a material disagreement or limitation of scope the audit opinion is modified by issuing a 'qualified with except for opinion'.
- When there is a pervasive disagreement, an adverse opinion is given.
- When there is a pervasive limitation of scope, a disclaimer of opinion is given.

# Chapter Overview

This chapter:

- explains the basic contents of an audit report;
- covers the potential modifications to audit reports:
  o   modifications to the opinion;
  o   emphasis of matter;
- discusses the effect of going concern on the audit report.

# 15. Audit Reports

## 15.1 THE AUDIT REPORT

The ultimate aim of the work performed by the auditor is to give an opinion on the Financial Statements and this opinion is contained in the **auditor's report**.

All audit reports follow a basic format, which is prescribed by the ISAs. However there is scope for individual countries to tailor the report format for their own purposes.

The advantages of a standardised format are:

* comparability between companies;
* the guarantee of a minimum level of content.

On the other hand, disadvantages of a standardised format are:

* the technical language used;
* auditors are restricted in terms of what they can actually say.

## 15.2 THE BASIC FORMAT OF THE AUDITOR'S REPORT

Each audit report contains the following elements:

| | |
|---|---|
| • **Title** | 'The Independent Auditor's Report'. The word 'independent' shows that the ethical requirements have been satisfied. |
| • **Addressee** | The report is addressed to the shareholders (i.e. the members). |
| • **Introduction** | States what has been audited i.e. the balance sheet, income statement, cash flow statements and notes. |
| • **Bannerman Paragraph (in the UK)** | States that the auditors only assume responsibility to the company and the shareholders and no other party that chooses to rely on the opinion. |
| • **Responsibilities of Directors and Auditors** | Clearly states the division of responsibilities in that directors are responsible for preparing the Financial Statements and auditors are responsible for expressing an opinion on them. |
| • **Basis of Opinion** | Details how the audit was carried out in order to arrive at the opinion. |
| • **Opinion** | Here auditors say whether or not the Financial Statements present a true and fair view and are properly prepared. |
| • **Signature and address of the auditors and the date that the report was signed.** | The report must contain the auditor's signature, detail their location and be dated. |

The report below is an example of a United Kingdom auditor's report.

## Independent Auditor's Report to the Members of ABC Plc

We have audited the Financial Statements of ABC Plc for the year ended [DATE], which comprise the Income Statement, the Statement of Financial Position, the Cash Flow Statement and the related notes. The accounting policies have been prepared under the accounting policies set out therein.

This report is made solely to the company's members, as a body, in accordance with the Companies Act 2006.

Our audit work has been undertaken so that we might state to the company's members those matters we are required to state to them in an auditor's report and for no other purpose. To the fullest extent permitted by law, we do not accept or assume responsibility to anyone other than the company and the company's members as a body, for our audit work, for this report, or for the opinions we have formed.

## Respective Responsibilities of Directors and Auditors

The directors' responsibilities for preparing the annual report and the Financial Statements in accordance with applicable law and United Kingdom accounting standards ('United Kingdom Generally Accepted Accounting Practice') are set out in the statement of directors' responsibilities.

Our responsibility is to audit the Financial Statements in accordance with relevant legal and regulatory requirements and International Standards on Auditing (UK and Ireland).

We report to you our opinion as to whether the Financial Statements give a true and fair view and have been properly prepared in accordance with the Companies Act 2006. We also report to you if, in our opinion, the company has not kept proper accounting records, if we have not received all the information and explanations we require for our audit, or if information specified by law regarding director's remuneration and other transactions is not disclosed.

We read the other information contained in the annual report and consider whether it is consistent with the audited Financial Statements. The other information comprises only the chairman's statement, the directors' report, the business review and the financial highlights. We consider the implication for our report if we become aware of any apparent misstatements or material inconsistencies with the Financial Statements. Our responsibilities do not extend to any other information. We report to you whether in our opinion the information given in the directors' report is consistent with the Financial Statements.

## Basis of Audit Opinion

We conducted our audit in accordance with International Standards on Auditing (UK and Ireland) issued by the Auditing Practices Board. An audit includes examination, on a test basis, of evidence relevant to the amounts and disclosures in the Financial Statements. It also includes an assessment of the significant estimates and judgements made by the directors in the preparation of the Financial Statements, and of whether the accounting policies are appropriate to the company's circumstances, consistently applied and adequately disclosed.

We planned and performed our audit so as to obtain all the information and explanations we considered necessary in order to provide us with sufficient evidence to give reasonable assurance that the Financial Statements are free material misstatement, whether caused by fraud or other irregularity or error. In forming our opinion we also evaluated the overall adequacy of the presentation of the information in the Financial Statements.

The information in the directors' report includes that specific information presented in the business review and the financial highlights that is cross-referenced from the 'review of the business' section of the directors' report.

*continues on next page*

---

**Opinion**

In our opinion:

The Financial Statements give a true and fair view, in accordance with United Kingdom Generally Accepted Accounting Practice, of the state of the company's affairs as at [YEAR END DATE] and of its profit (loss) for the year then ended.

The Financial Statements have been properly prepared in accordance with the Companies Act 2006.

**Auditor's name**
**Auditor's address**
**Date of audit report**

---

15.3    MODIFICATION TO THE AUDIT REPORT

An unmodified report is one that contains the standard wording (as above).

A modified report is any change from this standard wording and arises when:

*   The auditor needs to **change the opinion**, or
*   There is no need to change the opinion but the auditor wishes to add an **emphasis of matter paragraph** into the report.

We shall consider each in turn.

15.3.1  *MODIFYING THE AUDIT OPINION*

Certain issues may arise during the audit that result in the auditor needing to modify the audit opinion (i.e. a problem may arise suggesting that the Financial Statements are not true and fair or properly prepared).

Before deciding upon which opinion to give the auditor needs to consider:

1.  The **nature** of the problem; and
2.  The **materiality** of the problem.

15.3.2  *NATURE OF THE PROBLEM*

There are two main types of problem, which can give rise to a modification of the opinion:

Disagreement:          This is where the auditors audit a balance or disclosure and disagree with the client. The client however refuses to change the balance or disclosure.

Limitation of Scope:   This type of problem arises when the auditor is unable to audit a balance or disclosure because evidence that should be available isn't available.

15.3.3  *MATERIALITY OF THE PROBLEM*

Once the nature of the problem has been identified, the auditor determines the materiality of the problem and this in turn determines the audit opinion.

15.3.4  *DISAGREEMENTS*

| Size of Disagreement | Example | Audit Opinion |
|---|---|---|
| Immaterial Disagreements. | The auditor has audited the company's sundry expenses and disagrees with the client by $100. | The opinion will be **unmodified** as we are not concerned about an immaterial problem.<br>The opinion states that the Financial Statements are true and fair and properly prepared. |
| Material Disagreements. | The auditor has audited trade receivables and disagrees with the client's figure by $75,000. Total sales revenue is $1,500,000. | The opinion will be **modified**.<br>In this case, we use a particular type of modification called **'qualified with except for'**.<br>This opinion says that 'the Financial Statements are true and fair **except for** receivables'.<br>The auditors will also disclose the true value of receivables in the audit report. |
| Pervasive Disagreements. | The auditor has audited revenue and concludes it should be stated as $1,000,000. The client is saying $5,000,000. | The opinion will be **modified**.<br>A pervasive problem is one that is so serious, that unless it is corrected, the Financial Statements cannot possibly be true and fair.<br>In this case we use a modification known as an **adverse opinion**.<br>This opinion states that 'the Financial Statements are not true and fair'. |

## 15.3.5  *LIMITATIONS OF SCOPE*

| Size of Limitation | Example | Audit Opinion |
|---|---|---|
| Immaterial Limitation of Scope. | The auditor has not been able to audit window cleaning expenses for the finance department, as the receipts have been lost. | The opinion will be **unmodified** as we are not concerned about an immaterial problem.<br><br>The opinion states that the Financial Statements are true and fair and properly prepared. |
| Material Limitation of Scope. | The inventory records were destroyed in a warehouse fire before the end of the year. The client is stating that inventories are $245,000 out of gross assets of $4,900,000. The auditor is unable to substantiate this inventory balance. | The opinion will be **modified.** In this case, we use the particular type of modification called *'qualified with except for'*. This opinion says that 'the Financial Statements are true and fair **except for** inventories which we have not been able to audit'. |
| Pervasive Limitation of Scope. | The auditor's client is involved in the construction industry and most of its revenue comes from the construction of assets under long-term contracts. During the year they entered into a new contract making up 60% of their $900,000 revenue however they have not been able to provide any records of this contract. | The opinion will be **modified**. This problem is one that is so serious unless we obtain the required evidence, we cannot possibly say whether the Financial Statements are true and fair or not. In this case we use a modification known as a **Disclaimer of Opinion**. This opinion paragraph states that 'we cannot give an opinion on these Financial Statements'. |

This has all been summarised in the audit opinion flow chart below.

**The Audit Opinion Flow Chart**

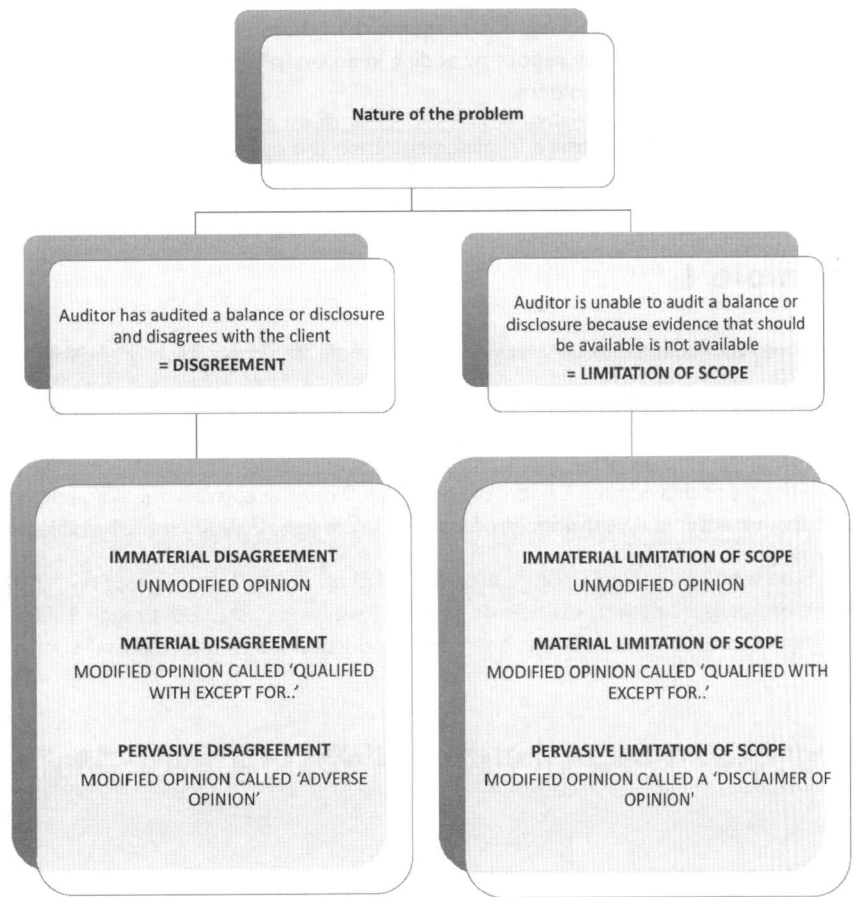

## 15.4 EMPHASIS OF MATTER PARAGRAPHS

There may be times where the Financial Statements are deemed to be true and fair and properly prepared, however, the auditor wishes to draw something **significant** to the shareholder's attention by adding in an emphasis of matter paragraph. This will also result in a modified audit report.

# Illustration

Benson Ltd has been accused by one of its customers of providing poor quality goods. As a result, the customer's production process was held up for a number of weeks and they are taking Benson to court to recoup some damages. The case was brought just before the year end and it is not expected to be settled for a few months.

Benson's lawyers have advised that there is a very high probability that the customer will win the case and Benson will be liable to pay damages of $1m. As a result, Benson have included a provision of $1m in the Financial Statements for the year and the auditors are satisfied, considering the probability, that accounting for a provision (rather than a contingent liability) is the correct treatment and that the amount is adequate.

As Benson have followed the correct accounting treatment there is no need to modify the audit opinion. However, as this is a significant and uncertain issue, as a matter of courtesy to the shareholders, the auditors should mention the provision in the audit report and they do this in an **emphasis of matter paragraph**.

## 15.5    GOING CONCERN AND THE AUDIT REPORT

If a company is experiencing doubts over its going concern status this must be disclosed in a note to the accounts.

If the auditors are happy that the disclosure is adequate then there is no need to modify the audit opinion, however, the auditors will modify the report by adding in an **emphasis of matter paragraph** to highlight this fundamental issue to the shareholders.

If the auditors believe that the disclosure is inadequate then the opinion will be modified due to a material disagreement.

# Learning Example 1

Determine whether or not the auditors will modify the audit report for each of the following scenarios:

1. Jones Limited did not carry out an inventory count at the year end and have insufficient records to support their stock valuation of $4m. Revenue was $50m and profit before tax $15m.

2. Scott Limited did not provide for a bad debt of $50,000 despite the fact that the customer went into administration just after the year end. Profit before tax was $500,000 and receivables was $200,000.

3. Phillips Limited is being sued by a competitor for the theft of intellectual property. The lawyers believe that this important, but not vital, case could go either way and costs could reach $500,000. The matter is material and a contingent liability has been disclosed in a note to the Financial Statements.

# Solution to Learning Example 1

1. JONES LIMITED

   **Nature of the Problem**
   Limitation of scope due to lack of evidence over inventory valuation and quantity.

   **Materiality**
   The value of the inventories is 8% of revenue and 27% of profit before tax so is considered to be material.

   **Opinion**
   A material limitation of scope will result in a modified opinion. The particular modification will be a 'qualification with an except for'.

2. SCOTT LIMITED

   **Nature of the Problem**
   This is a disagreement over a bad debt that should have been provided for (the bankruptcy of the customer is an adjusting post-balance sheet event).

   **Materiality**
   The value of the debt is 10% of revenue and 25% of receivables so is considered to be material.

   **Opinion**
   A material disagreement will result in a modified opinion. The particular modification will be a 'qualification with an except for'.

3. PHILLIPS LIMITED

   **Nature of the Problem**
   The lawyers have indicated that the case could go either way therefore it should be considered 'possible' that Phillips will lose. As a result, Phillips should be disclosing a contingent liability and they have done this.

   **Materiality**
   It is stated that the matter is material to the Financial Statements.

   **Opinion**
   There is no need to modify the opinion as Phillips has followed the correct accounting treatment. However, the auditors will modify the report by adding in an emphasis of matter paragraph to highlight the case.

# Learning summary

- Make sure you can reproduce the audit opinion flowchart without reference to the notes.
- Read the ACCA student article 'Ready to sit paper F8?' and 'Audit and Assurance Assistance'.
  **http://www.accaglobal.com/students/publications/student_accountant/archive/2008/90/3150174**
  **http://www.accaglobal.com/students/publications/student_accountant/archive/2008/85/3086589**

# F8

Index

London
School of Business
& Finance
shaping success in business and finance

F8

Feedback
and
Review Form

Please take the time to complete this feedback and review form about the study materials that you have used for your ACCA exams. We really appreciate your comments.

## YOUR DETAILS

Name    :

Address   :

How did you use this material?

- ☐    Home study (only using books)
- ☐    Home study (books and InterActive videos)
- ☐    Classroom course

What made you buy this material?

- ☐    Saw information on LSBF website
- ☐    Saw information on InterActive website
- ☐    Saw advertisement
- ☐    Recommendation from friend/colleague
- ☐    Recommended by lecturer at college
- ☐    Used LSBF/InterActive materials before
- ☐    Other (please state)

## STUDY MANUALS

Please make an assessment about the quality of the videos were in the following areas:

|  | Very useful | Useful | Not useful |
|---|---|---|---|
| Clarity of tutor explanations | ☐ | ☐ | ☐ |
| Engaging and interesting tutor | ☐ | ☐ | ☐ |
| Exam focus, hints and tips | ☐ | ☐ | ☐ |
| Examples and exercises | ☐ | ☐ | ☐ |
| Overall Opinion | ☐ | ☐ | ☐ |

Would you use our materials again?

☐    Yes    ☐    No

## INTERACTIVE VIDEOS (IF USED)

Please make an assessment about the quality of the videos were in the following areas:

|  | Very useful | Useful | Not useful |
|---|---|---|---|
| Clarity of tutor explanations | ☐ | ☐ | ☐ |
| Engaging and interesting tutor | ☐ | ☐ | ☐ |
| Exam focus, hints and tips | ☐ | ☐ | ☐ |
| Examples and exercises | ☐ | ☐ | ☐ |
| Overall opinion | ☐ | ☐ | ☐ |

Please return this form to: Paul Merison, Publications Manager, London School of Business and Finance, 8-9 Holborn, London ECIN 2LL.

Please use this space to make any additional comments that you have about either the InterActive videos, study manuals or any other aspect of our service:

Thank you for taking your time to complete this form. Good luck in your forthcoming exams.

If you would like to make any other general comments about this manual, please forward them to **feedback@studyinteractive.org** or complete our electronic feedback on **www.lsbf.org.uk/pbfeedback**